To Emma. Star Chart Prize December 1987

J. Paintin.

Orbis Publishing, London

The Peacock King

MADAME D'AULNOY

The Peacock King

and other stories

Illustrated by Albín Brunovský

ORBIS PUBLISHING,
LONDON

Translation by Annie Macdonell and Miss Lee
Illustrations © 1980 by Albín Brunovský
This edition © 1985 Orbis Publishing Limited, London
Graphic design Ľubomír Krátky
This illustrated selection was first published in 1980 by Mladé letá, Bratislava

Printed in Czechoslovakia
ISBN 0-85613-791-X

CONTENTS

Prince Ariel

ONCE upon a time there lived a king and a queen who had only one son, of whom they were passionately fond, though he was a very ill-shapen boy. He was as stout as the biggest man and as short as the tiniest dwarf. But the ugliness of his face and the deformity of his body were as nothing compared to his evil disposition. He was a self-willed little wretch, and a nuisance to everybody. From his earliest childhood the king had noticed this, but the queen was foolishly blind to his faults, and helped to spoil him still more by her excessive indulgence, which let him plainly see the power he had over her. To gain favour with this lady you had but to tell her that her son was handsome and clever. She wished to give him a name that would inspire respect and fear, and after racking her brains for a long time she called him Furibon.

When he was old enough to have a tutor, the king chose for this purpose a prince who had ancient claims on the crown, and who would have maintained them like a man of spirit, if his affairs had been in a better state. But he had long given up all thought of this, and his whole time was occupied with the education of his only son. Never was there a lad gifted with a finer nature, a quicker or keener mind, or a gentler, meeker spirit. Everything he said had a happy turn and a special grace of its own, and in his person he was charming. The king having chosen this great lord to be the guide of Furibon's youth, told his son to be very obedient, but Furibon was a naughty urchin to whom a hundred floggings made no difference. The tutor's son was called Leander, and everybody liked him. The ladies looked on him with much interest, but as he paid no special attention to any of them, they called him the Fair

Indifferent. And they laid siege to him to make him change his manner towards them, but for all that he hardly ever left Furibon. Furibon, however, only seemed to them the more hideous now that he appeared side by side with Leander, for he never came near the ladies except to say rude things to them: sometimes to tell them they were badly dressed, or that they were like country cousins, or—and this before everybody—that their faces were painted. He would get to know their secrets, only to tell them to the queen, who scolded them, and as a punishment cut short their rations. All this made them hate Furibon with a deadly hatred. He knew it, and he took his revenge on young Leander. "You are very lucky," he said, looking at him sulkily. "The ladies are always praising you, but they behave very differently to me." "My lord," said Leander, modestly, "the respect they have for you prevents their being on such familiar terms." "It is just as well for them they do feel so," Furibon said; "for otherwise I would beat them to a jelly to teach them their duty."

One day, when ambassadors from a far country were expected, the prince and Leander were waiting in a gallery to see them go past. As soon as the ambassadors saw Leander they came forward and made profound bows before him, showing in every way their admiration. Then, looking at Furibon, thinking he must be the prince's dwarf, they took him by the arm, and twirled him round and round in spite of himself. Leander was in despair. He made every effort to make them understand that it was the king's son they were treating in this fashion. They did not know what he was saying, and unfortunately the interpreter had gone to await them by the king. Leander, seeing that they did not understand his signs, humbled himself still more before Furibon, and the ambassadors and their suite, thinking he was playing, laughed like to split their sides, and wanted to tweak the prince by the nose, after the fashion of their country. Furibon, in a towering rage, drew his little sword, which was no longer than a fan, and would have attacked them if the king had not come at that moment to meet the ambassadors, and been a witness to this violent scene. He apologised to them, for he knew their tongue, but they answered that it was of no consequence, for they had seen very well that the hideous little dwarf was in a bad temper. The king was much distressed that the ugly face and the violence of his son should prevent his being recognised. When the king and the ambassadors were out of sight Furibon took Leander by the hair, and plucked out two or three handfuls, and he would have strangled him if he had been able. Then he told him never again to come into his presence. Leander's father, very angry at what Furibon had done, sent his son away to a castle he had in the country. There he never found time hang heavy on his hands, for he was fond of hunting, fishing, and walking. He could paint; he read a great deal, and could play on several instruments. He thought himself lucky no longer to have to pay court to the eccentric prince, and in spite of his being all by himself he was never lonely.

One day when he had been walking for a long time in his gardens, the heat becoming very great, he went into a little wood where the trees were tall and the foliage thick, to enjoy the pleasant shade. He began playing the flute to amuse himself, when he felt something turning round his leg and gripping it very tight. He looked to see what it could be, and was much astonished to find a great adder. Taking his handkerchief he seized it by the head, and was just going to kill it when the creature twisted the rest of its body round his arm, and fixed its eyes on him as if asking for mercy. One of his gardeners came up at that moment, and no sooner had he seen the adder than he cried out to his master: "My lord, hold it fast. For a whole hour I have been running after it trying to kill it. It is the slyest beast in the world, and ruins our flower beds." Leander cast his eyes again on the adder. It was spotted all over with a thousand different colours. It looked at him still fixedly, but made not a movement to defend itself. "Since you wished to kill it," he said to his gardener, "and it has come to take refuge with me, I forbid you to hurt it in any way. I wish to feed it, and when it has cast off its beautiful skin I shall let it go." Then he went back to his castle, and put it in a large room of which he kept the key, and sent bran, and milk, and flowers, and herbs to feed it and make it happy. What a lucky snake! Sometimes he would go to see it, and as soon as it caught sight of him it came to meet him, crawling along and putting on all the little airs and graces an adder is capable of. The prince was very much surprised, yet he paid no great attention to the matter.

Meanwhile all the ladies of the court were grieved at Leander's absence, and their talk was of nothing but him and of how they wished he were back again. "Alas!" they said, " there is no more pleasure at the court since Leander has gone, and it is all the fault of that wicked Furibon. Why should he be jealous because Leander is handsomer and more beloved than himself? Must Leander, to please him, disfigure his shape and his face? Must he dislocate his bones to be like him, or split his mouth from ear to ear, or close up his fine eyes, or cut off his nose? What an unreasonable little wretch! He will never be happy his whole life long, for he will never find anyone who is not handsomer than himself."

But however wicked princes may be, they always have flatterers—and, in fact, wicked princes have even more than others. So it was with Furibon. His power over the mind of the queen made him formidable. When he heard what the ladies said he was mad with rage, and going to the queen's room he told her he would kill himself before her face if she did not find some means of putting Leander to death. The queen, who hated Leander because he was handsomer than her monkey of a son, replied that she had long looked upon him as a traitor, and that with a right good will she would have a hand in his death. So he planned that he would go hunting with those favourites whom he could put most trust in, and that when Leander joined them they would teach him what comes of people worming themselves into everybody's favour. Furibon, therefore, went a-hunting. When Leander heard the dogs and the horns in his woods, he mounted his horse and rode out to

see what was happening. When he saw the prince he was very much surprised and, dismounting, he saluted him respectfully. Furibon received him better than he expected, and told him to follow him. Then, turning round, he made a sign to the assassins not to fail in their attack. He himself was riding off at full speed when a lion of an enormous size came out of the depths of its cavern, and rushing on him, threw him to the ground. Those who were with him ran away. Leander alone remained to face the furious animal. Advancing with his sword in his hand, at the risk of being devoured, by his valour and his dexterity he saved his most cruel enemy. Furibon had fainted from fright. Leander tended him in the most careful fashion, and when he had recovered consciousness, he set him on his own horse. Anyone but a thankless wretch would have felt grateful to the very depths of his soul for so great and recent a service, and by word and deed would

have shown his gratitude. Not so Furibon. He did not even look at Leander, and only used his horse to go and seek the assassins, whom he again ordered to kill his preserver. They therefore surrounded Leander, who must certainly have been killed had his courage been less. Making for a tree, he leant up against it so as not to be attacked from behind, and, sparing none of his enemies, he fought desperately. Furibon, thinking he was dead, hastened up to have the pleasure of looking on his dead body, but a very different scene from what he expected met his eyes, for the whole gang of villains were breathing their last. When Leander saw him, he came forward and said: "My lord, if it is by your order that they attempted to murder me, I am sorry I resisted." "Get you gone with your insolence," replied the prince, in wrath. "If ever you appear before me again I will put you to death."

Leander made no reply, and, sad at heart, he made his way home. The night was spent in thinking what he should do, for there seemed no likelihood of his being able to successfully resist the king's son; so he made up his mind to travel over the whole world. But just when he was ready to set off, he remembered the adder, and went to take it some milk and fruit. As he was opening the door, he saw a strange light shining in one of the corners of the room. Looking more closely, he was much astonished to see a lady, whose noble and majestic presence gave evidence of her high rank. Her dress was of amaranth satin, embroidered with diamonds and pearls. Coming forward with a gracious air, she said to him: "Young prince, do not seek here for the adder you brought hither. It is here no longer, and you find me in its place to pay you its debt. But to speak more plainly: well, I am Fairy Gentille, famous for the many merry and dexterous tricks I know how to perform. All our family live for a hundred years without growing old. We are never ill: we have no sorrows or pains. That time over, we become adders for eight days. It is this period alone that is dangerous for us, for then we can neither foresee nor prevent any misfortunes that may happen to us; and if we are killed we never live again. The eight

days past, we assume once more our ordinary shape, our beauty, our power, and our treasures. Now you understand, my lord, what I owe you, and it is only just that I should pay my debt. Think, therefore, what would be useful to you, and be sure of my good will." The young prince, who up to this time had had no dealings with the fairies, was so filled with astonishment that it was long before he could speak. But, making her a low bow, he said: "Madam, after the honour that has been mine in serving you, fortune has nothing left to give me." "I should be very sorry," she said, "were you not to give me a chance of being useful to you. Think a little, for I can make you a great king. I can prolong your life; make you even handsomer than you are; give you mines of diamonds, and houses full of gold. I can make you a fine orator, a poet, a musician, a painter. I can give you favour in the ladies' eyes: I can give you a fuller intelligence. I can turn you into a spirit of the air, the water, and the earth." Here Leander interrupted her. "Forgive me for asking, madam," he said, "but what would be the good of being a spirit?" "Why, it would have all kinds of uses and delights," replied the fairy. "You could cross in a moment the vast plains of the universe. You could mount into the air without wings. You could visit the depths of the earth without being dead; sound the abysses of the sea without being drowned: gain entrance everywhere though the windows and the doors be shut. Then, whenever you liked, you could take your own natural shape again." "Ah, madam!" he cried, "I should like to be such a spirit. I am on the point of setting out on my travels, and I can imagine the infinite delight which I could enjoy with the powers you describe, and I prefer this gift to all those you have so generously offered to me." "Then," replied Gentille, passing her hand three times over his eyes and face, "henceforth be Ariel, Ariel the beloved, Ariel the beautiful, Ariel the merry." She kissed him, and gave him a little red hat, decked with parrots' feathers. "When you put on this hat," she said, "you will be invisible; when you take it off you will be visible."

Leander, in great delight, clapped the little red hat on his head, and wished that he might go into the forest and pick the wild roses he had seen there. At that moment his body became light as thought. He was transported into the forest, passing through the window and flying like a bird. He could not help feeling afraid when he saw himself so high in the air, and when he was above a river he feared he might fall into it without the fairy having the power of preventing it. But he found himself safely at the foot of the rose tree, and plucking three roses, he returned at once to the room where the fairy still was. He presented them to her, full of delight that his little trial trip had succeeded so well. But she told him to keep the roses: that one of them would supply him with all the money he would need; that if he put the second on his mistress's throat he would know if she loved him truly; and that the third would prevent his falling ill. Then, without waiting for his thanks, she wished him bon voyage and vanished.

He was greatly delighted with the fine gift he had just received. "Could I ever have thought," he said, "that saving a poor snake from the hands of my gardener would have brought me such a wonderful, such a splendid reward? Oh, how happy I shall be! What a pleasant time I shall have! How much I shall learn! When I am invisible I can find out the greatest secrets." It passed through his mind, too, that he should very much enjoy taking vengeance on Furibon. Setting his affairs hastily in order, he mounted the finest horse in his stable, which was called Grisdelin, and ordered some of his servants in his own livery to follow him, in order that the news of his return to court might the sooner get abroad.

Now you must know that Furibon, who was a great liar, had reported that had it not been for his own bravery, Leander would have murdered him while they were out hunting, that he had killed all his men, and that he must be brought to justice. The king, urged by the queen, ordered him to be arrested, so that when Leander came to court in this bold fashion, Furibon was warned of his

arrival. He was too timid to go to meet him himself; but running to his mother's room, he told her that Leander had just come, and begged her to have him seized. The queen, ever eager to fulfil the least desire of her miserable son, set off at once to find the king, and the prince, impatient to know the decision, followed her in silence. Stopping at the door, he leaned his ear to the keyhole, putting his hair aside so as to hear the better. Meanwhile Leander came into the great hall of the palace wearing his little red hat, which, of course, made him invisible. When he saw Furibon listening he took a hammer and nail and nailed his ear fast to the door. Furibon, desperate, raging with pain, knocked at the door like a madman, shrieking loudly. At his voice the queen ran to open the door, and in doing so tore off the prince's ear, which made him bleed as if he had been murdered, and caused him to make faces horrible to see. The queen, inconsolable, took him on her knee, and taking the ear in her hand, kissed it and stuck it on again. Ariel seized a bunch of rods that were used for beating the king's little dogs, and with these he rapped the queen's knuckles and her son's nose several times. She shrieked out that she was being murdered, massacred. The king looked everywhere. Everybody ran hither and thither, but no one was to be seen, and they whispered that the queen must be mad from the grief of seeing Furibon's ear torn off. It was the king who first thought so, and when she came near him he moved out of her way. It was a very funny scene! At last, after Ariel had given Furibon a good beating, he left the room, and went into the garden, where he made himself visible again. Here he openly plucked the cherries, the apricots, the strawberries, and the flowers from the queen's beds. She used to water these herself, and it was as much as anyone's life was worth to touch them. The gardeners, very much surprised, came and told their majesties that Prince Leander was robbing the trees of their fruit and the garden of its flowers. "What insolence!" cried the queen. "My little Furibon, my own darling, forget for a moment your hurt, and run after this villain. Take the guards, the musketeers, the policemen, the courtiers. Place yourself at their head, seize him, and cut him to pieces." Furibon, fired by his mother's words, and followed by a thousand well-armed men, entered the garden, and saw Leander under a tree. Leander threw a stone at Furibon and broke his arm, and he pelted the rest of the troop with oranges. They rushed towards him, but lo! at that moment he had disappeared. Stepping behind Furibon, who was already in a sorry plight, he passed a cord through his legs, which threw him on his nose. The prince was picked up and taken home to bed, very ill.

Leander, satisfied with this revenge, returned to his attendants who were waiting for him and, giving them money, he sent them back to his castle, not wishing to take anyone with him who might know the secret of the little red hat and the roses. Not having made up his mind where he wished to go, he mounted his beautiful horse Grisdelin and let it go at its will. He passed through countless woods, over plains, hills and valleys, resting now and again, eating and sleeping, without meeting any remarkable adventure. At last he reached a forest, where he stopped to enjoy the shade for a little, for it was very hot. After a moment he heard the sound of sighing and sobbing and, looking round everywhere, he saw a man running, then stopping, now crying out, now saying nothing for a while, tearing his hair, beating his body, till Leander had no doubt but that he was some miserable person who had lost his wits. He seemed to be handsome and young. His clothes had once been splendid, but now they were all tattered. The prince, moved with compassion, addressed him: "I see you in so unhappy a condition that I cannot help asking you what is the matter and offering you my services." "Ah! my lord," replied the young man, "there is no remedy for my ills. To-day my dear mistress is going to be sacrificed to a jealous old wretch, who is rich in the world's goods, but who will make her the unhappiest creature in the whole world!" "She loves you then?" said Leander. "I may flatter myself she does," he answered. "And where is she?" said the prince. "In a castle at the farther end of this forest," replied the lover. "Very

well, wait for me," said Leander again. "I will bring you good news before very long." And so saying, he put on the little red hat, and wished himself in the castle. He had not reached it before he heard the sound of beautiful music; and, on entering, the whole palace resounded with the noise of violins and other instruments. He made his way into a great hall thronged with the relatives and friends of the old man and the young damsel. Nothing could have been lovelier than she was, but the pallor of her complexion, the sadness in her face, and the tears that flooded her eyes from time to time, were quite enough to show her suffering.

Leander, who had now turned into the invisible Ariel, remained in a corner to watch some of those who were present. He saw the father and mother of the pretty maiden, who were scolding her for the discontented face she was wearing. When they had returned to their places, Ariel stationed himself behind the mother, and whispered in her ear: "Since you force your daughter to give her hand to this old villain, know for certain that before eight days are over you will be punished by death." The woman, terrified at hearing a voice and seeing no one, and still more at the threat which had been uttered, screamed aloud and fell down on the floor. Her husband asked what was the matter, and she cried out that she was a dead woman if her daughter's marriage took place, and that for all the riches of the world she would not permit it. The husband laughed at her, and told her she was dreaming; but Ariel, going up to him, said: "Old sceptic, if you do not believe what your wife says, you will pay for your doubt with your life. Break off your daughter's wedding, and give her up at once to the man she loves." These words produced a wonderful effect. Without more ado they despatched the bridegroom, telling him they would not have broken off the match but for orders from on high. He did not believe what they said, and would have sought to gain his end by trickery, for he was a Norman; but Ariel shouted so loud in his ear that he was nearly deafened, and to make sure of his departure, he trod so hard on his gouty feet that he nearly squeezed them flat. So they ran to seek for the lover in the wood, who in the meanwhile was in despair. Ariel was waiting for him with the utmost impatience, only less than that of his young mistress. The lover and his bride nearly died of joy. The feast prepared for the old man's wedding served for the happy lovers, and Ariel, taking his human shape again, appeared suddenly at the hall door in the guise of a stranger drawn thither by the noise of the feast. As soon as the bridegroom saw him, he ran and threw himself at his feet, calling him every name that his gratitude could suggest to him. Leander spent two days in this castle, and if he had liked he might have ruined them, for they offered him all they possessed; and he did not quit such good company without regret.

Going on his way, he reached a large city where lived a queen whose great desire was to gather about her court all the handsomest persons in her kingdom. Leander on his arrival had the finest equipage prepared that ever was seen; for, after all, he had only to shake the rose, and money never failed him. It is easy to imagine that being handsome, young, witty, and, above all, splendid in appearance, the queen and all the princesses received him with every mark of respect and consideration.

This was the most gallant court in the whole world, and not to be in love there was to be laughed at. So wishing to follow the custom, he thought he would play at falling in love, and that when he went away he could leave his love behind him as easily as his suite. And he cast his eyes on one of the queen's maids-of-honour, called Fair Blondine. This lady was very clever, but so cold and so serious that he did not know very well what to do to please her. He arranged wonderful fêtes, and balls, and plays every night. He sent for rarities from all parts of the world, but it seemed to have no effect on her. Still, the more indifferent she was, the more was he determined to gain her favour. What chiefly attracted him was that he believed she had never loved anyone else. But to be certain he thought he should like to try on her the power of the rose. So, as if playfully, he placed it on Blondine's bosom, when suddenly,

fresh and blooming as it had been, it withered and faded. That was enough to let Leander know that he had a rival whom she loved. He felt this very keenly, and to be convinced of it by his own eyes, he wished himself in Blondine's room in the evening. There he saw a musician come in who had the most villainous face imaginable. This man screeched out three or four couplets he had made for her, the words and the music of which were alike detestable, but she enjoyed them as if they were the finest things she had ever heard in her life. He made faces as if he were possessed, and even these she praised, so mad about him was she; and at last she let this hideous wretch kiss her hand as a reward. Ariel, enraged, threw himself on this impertinent musician; and pushing him roughly against a balcony, flung him into the garden, where he broke his few remaining teeth.

If a thunderbolt had fallen on Blondine she could not have been more surprised. She thought it must be the work of some spirit. Ariel vanished from the room without showing himself, and at once returned to his own quarters, where he wrote to Blondine, heaping on her all the reproaches she deserved. Without awaiting her answer he set off, leaving behind him his equipage, which he presented to his squires and his gentlemen, and rewarding the rest of his people. Then mounting on his trusty Grisdelin, he made up his mind never to fall in love again after what had happened. He set out at full speed. For a long time he was very melancholy, but his good sense and absence from Blondine came to his aid in time. On his arrival in another town he learnt that a great ceremony was to take place that day, on the occasion of the admission of a maiden among the vestal virgins, though she had no wish to be one. The prince was much touched when he heard of this. He felt that the little red hat had only been given him to repair public wrongs and to comfort the distressed. So he hastened to the temple. There the young girl was crowned with flowers, dressed in white, and her long hair fell over her like a mantle. Two of her brothers led her by the hand, and her mother followed her with a great company of men and women. The eldest vestal was waiting for her at the temple door. At that moment Ariel called out: "Stop, stop, wicked brethren, cruel mother, stop! heaven will not consent to this wrong being done. If you go on you will be trampled to death like frogs." They looked round everywhere without finding out where the terrible threats were coming from. The brothers said it must be their sister's lover who was hiding at the bottom of some hole to play the oracle, but Ariel, flying into a rage, took a long stick and beat them soundly. You could see the stick rise and fall about their shoulders like a hammer on an anvil, and the blows at least were real enough. The vestals were seized with terror, and fled, the others following. Ariel remained with the young victim. Taking off his little hat, he asked her in what way he could help her. She told him, with more courage than could have been expected of a girl of her age, that there was a knight whom she cared for very much, but who was poor. Then he shook Fairy Gentille's rose so vigorously that he shot out ten million pounds for her and her lover. The two young people got married, and lived happy ever afterwards.

The last adventure he had was the best of all. Entering a great forest he heard the piteous cries of a young maiden, who he had no doubt was being hurt in some way. Looking all around he saw four men, fully armed, bearing away a damsel who seemed to be about thirteen or fourteen years of age. Advancing as speedily as possible, he cried out: "What has this child done that you should treat her as a slave?" "And what is that to you, my little lordling?" said he who seemed to be the leader of the band. "I command you," said Leander, "to let her go at once." "Oh, certainly, certainly!" they answered, laughing. In great wrath the prince dismounted, and put on the little red hat, for he did not think it would be wise to attack all by himself four men strong enough to be a match for twelve. When he had on his little hat you would have been very clever if you could have seen him. The robbers said: "He is gone. Don't let us mind about him. Seize his horse only." One stopped to guard the young damsel, while the other three ran after

Grisdelin, who gave them no end of trouble. "Alas, fair princess!" said the girl, "how happy I was in your palace! How can I live without you? If you knew what has happened to me, you would send your Amazons after poor Abricotine." Leander listened, and without a moment's delay he seized the arm of the robber who kept the girl, and tied it to a tree before he had the time to defend himself, for he did not even know who it was that had bound him. At his cries one of his comrades came running up out of breath and asked him who had tied him to the tree. "I do not know. I have seen no one." "That is only an excuse," said the other. "But I have known for long that you were nothing but a coward, and I shall treat you as you deserve." Thereupon he belaboured him with his stirrup leathers. Ariel was much amused to hear him screaming.

Then going up to the second robber he took him by the arm, and fastened him also to a tree, just opposite his comrade, not forgetting to ask him: "Well, my good fellow, and who has dared to attack you? Are you not a great coward to have permitted it?" The man answered not a word, but bent his head for shame, unable to imagine how he had been tied to the tree without seeing anyone.

Meanwhile Abricotine took the opportunity of running away, without even knowing where she was going. Leander no longer seeing her, called out to Grisdelin, and the horse, eager to find his master, freed himself by two kicks from the robbers who had caught him, breaking the head of one and three ribs of the other. The first thing to be done now was to rejoin Abricotine, for Ariel thought her very pretty, and he wished to be in the young damsel's company. In a moment he had reached her, and found her so very, very tired that she was leaning up against a tree, hardly able to stand. When she saw Grisdelin coming along so gaily, she cried out: "What good luck! Here is a pretty horse to carry Abricotine to the Palace of Delights." Ariel heard what she said, but she did not see him. He went up to her; Grisdelin stopped; and she sprang on his back. Ariel clasped her in his arms, and set her gently in front of him. Oh! how terrified Abricotine was to feel someone there, and yet to see nobody! She dared not move, and she shut her eyes for fear she should see a spirit, and did not utter a syllable. The prince, who had always his pockets full of the nicest sugar-plums in the world, tried to put some in her mouth, but she shut her teeth and lips quite tightly. At last, taking off his little hat, he said: "Why, Abricotine, you are a very timid girl to be so much afraid of me. It was I who saved you out of the robbers' hands." Then she opened her eyes and recognised him. "Ah! my lord," she said, "I owe you everything. It is true I was terrified at being in the company of someone whom I could not see." "I am not invisible," he replied; "but you have evidently hurt your eyes, and you could not therefore see me." Abricotine believed him, though for all that she was sharp enough as a rule. After talking for some time on things in

general, Leander begged her to tell him her age, where her home was, and by what mischance she had fallen into the bandits' hands. "I owe you too much," she said, "not to satisfy your curiosity; but, my lord, I beg you to give less attention to my story than to the means of getting on our way speedily."

"A fairy, who surpassed every other in fairy lore," began Abricotine, "fell so madly in love with a certain prince that, though she was the first of her race who had been so weak, she married him, in spite of all persuasions to the contrary from the other fairies, who placed before her ceaselessly the wrong she was doing to their kind. They refused to let her live amongst them any longer, and all she could do was to build a great palace on the borders of their kingdom. But the prince whom she had married got tired of her. He was much annoyed because she had the power of seeing all his actions; and as soon as he showed the least favour to any other lady she made a terrible commotion, and would revenge herself on the prettiest damsel in the world by making her hideously ugly. The prince, feeling very discomfited by such an inconvenient amount of affection, set off one fine morning with fast horses, and journeyed a long, long way off, to hide himself in a big hole in the depths of a mountain, in order that she might not be able to find him. It was no use. She followed him, and, telling him that a child was about to be born, begged him to return to his palace; that she would give him money, and horses, and dogs, and arms; that she would have a riding-school built, and a tennis-court and a mall made for his amusement. All this had no effect on him, for by nature he was very obstinate and fond of lawless pleasures. He said all sorts of rude things to her, and called her an old surly witch. 'It is very lucky for you,' she said, 'that my good temper is greater than your folly, otherwise I would turn you into a cat, and you should pass your life mewling on the spout, or into a filthy toad, dabbling in the mud, or into a pumpkin, or an owl. But the worst I can possibly do is to leave you to your own folly. Stay here, then, in your hole, in your dark cave with the bears. Call the shepherdesses of the neighbourhood round you. In time you will get to know the difference between the low country folks and a fairy like me, who can be as charming as she likes.'

"With this she mounted on her flying car, and sped away as swift as a bird. As soon as she reached her home she transported her palace to an island, drove away her guards and her officers, took women of the Amazonian race and set them round her isle to keep a careful watch so that no men might ever set foot thereon. She called the spot the Isle of Calm Delights, and she used to say that no true pleasures were possible wherein men had any part. She bred up her daughter in this opinion. Never was there such a beautiful maiden. She is the princess I serve," continued Abricotine; "and, as pleasures reign where she is, no one grows old in her palace. To look at me you would not think it, but I am more than two hundred years old. When my mistress grew up her fairy mother left her her island; and having given her many lessons in the art of living a happy life, went back to the realm of Faërie once more. And the Princess of Calm Delights governs her state in an admirable fashion. I do not remember in all my life having seen any other men than those robbers who carried me off; and now you, my lord. Those men told me that they had been sent by a certain ugly, mis-shapen creature called Furibon, who loves my mistress, though he has only seen her portrait. They hung round the island without daring to set foot on it, for our Amazons are too watchful to let anyone land. But I have charge of the princess's birds, and I let a beautiful parrot escape, and fearing I should be scolded, I imprudently left the island to seek for it. So they caught me, and would have taken me away with them had it not been for your help."

"If you really feel grateful," said Leander, "may I not hope, fair Abricotine, that you will let me land on the Isle of Calm Delights, and let me see this wonderful princess who never grows old?" "Ah! my lord," she said, "we should be ruined, both you and I, if we did anything of the kind. It should be very easy for you to do

without a pleasure which you have never known. You have never been in this palace: imagine to yourself that it does not exist." "It is not so easy as you think," answered the prince, "to wipe out of one's memory the things that take kindly root there; and I do not agree with you that to banish our sex is a sure means of securing calm delights." "My lord," she replied, "it is not for me to decide. I even confess that if all men were like you I should be glad that the princess should make other laws; but having only seen five, four of whom were villains, I conclude that the wicked outnumber the good, and that it is therefore best to banish all of them."

While they were speaking they arrived at the banks of a great river. Abricotine jumped lightly to the ground. "Adieu, my lord," she said to the prince, making him a low bow; "I wish you so much happiness that the whole earth may be for you an island of delights. Now go away in haste, lest our Amazons see you." "And as for me," he answered, "fair Abricotine, I pray that a tender heart may be given you, so that some memory of me may remain with you." Then he went on his way. In the thickest part of a wood which he saw near the river he unharnessed Grisdelin, so that he might wander about and graze for a little. Putting on the little red hat, he wished himself in the Isle of Calm Delights. His wish was granted at once, and he found himself in a very beautiful and very extraordinary place. The palace was of pure gold, with figures on the roof of crystal and precious stones, representing the signs of the zodiac and all the wonders of nature—the sciences, the arts, the elements, the sea with its fish, the earth with its living things; Diana at the chase with her nymphs, the noble exercises of the Amazons, the amusements of a country life, shepherdesses with their flocks and their dogs; rustic labours, agriculture, harvesting, gardens, flowers, bees,—and yet amongst all those different things there was never the image of a man nor a boy, not even a little Cupid; for the fairy had been too angry with her disloyal husband to show favour to any of his unfaithful sex. "Abricotine has not deceived me," said the prince to himself. "The very idea of men has been banished from this place; let us see whether they lose much thereby. Entering the palace, at every step he took such wonderful things met his eyes that it was with great difficulty he could withdraw them again. The gold and the diamonds were wonderful, even more for their workmanship than for their intrinsic worth. Everywhere he met maidens of gentle look, innocent and merry, and fair as a sunny morning. Passing through endless vast rooms, he found some full of exqusite china vases, the odour from which, along with the odd colours and designs, delighted him greatly. Some of the rooms had walls of porcelain, so fine that you could see the light through them. Others were of engraved rock crystal, others of amber and coral, lapis lazuli,

agate, and cornelian, while the princess's room was all made of great mirrors, for so fair an object could not be too often seen. The throne was made of a single pearl, hollowed out like a shell, in which she sat with perfect ease. It was all hung round with branched candlesticks decked with rubies and diamonds. But this splendour was as nothing by the side of the incomparable beauty of the princess herself. Her childlike air had all the grace of youth with the dignity of a riper age. Nothing could equal the gentleness and the brightness of her eyes. In fact, it was impossible to find fault with her at any point. She was just then smiling graciously to her maids-of-honour, who that day had dressed themselves as nymphs for her amusement. Not seeing Abricotine, she asked where she was. The nymphs replied that they had sought her in vain. She was nowhere to be found. Ariel was dying to speak to her, and so he imitated the shrill little voice of a parrot (there were several in the room), and said: "Dear princess, Abricotine will come back soon. She was in great danger of being carried off, had not a young prince found her." "You are very pretty, my little parrot," she said, "but I think you are mistaken, and when Abricotine returns she will beat you." "I shall not be beaten," said Ariel, still in the parrot's voice. "She will tell you how much the stranger wished he might come into this palace, to root out from your mind your false ideas against his sex." "Really, my pretty poll," cried the princess, "it is quite a pity that you are not as amusing every day. I would love you dearly." "Ah! if I need only talk to please you," said Ariel, "I shall not stop talking for a minute." "Well, now," said the princess, "would you not certainly say this parrot was a wizard?" "He is too much of a lover to be a wizard," he answered.

At that moment Abricotine entered; and throwing herself at her fair mistress's feet, she told her adventure, and painted the prince's portrait in the brightest and most pleasing colours. "I should have hated all men," she added, "if I had not seen him. Ah! madam, how charming he is! In his look and his whole manner

there is something noble and spiritual and, as everything he says is most fascinating, I think I have done wisely in not bringing him here." The princess made no answer to this, but went on questioning Abricotine about the prince, as to his name, his country, his birth, where he came from, where he was going to. Afterwards she fell into a deep reverie. Ariel watched everything, and continued to speak in the same voice. "Abricotine is an ungrateful girl, madam," he said. "This poor stranger will die of grief if he does not see you." "Very well, poll, let him die; and, since you take upon yourself to talk seriously, I forbid you ever to speak to me again of that unknown prince."

Leander was delighted to see that Abricotine's story and the parrot's had made such an impression on the princess, and he looked at her with a pleasure which made him forget his former vows never to fall in love in his life—for there was no comparison between her and the vain Blondine. "Is it possible," he said to himself, "that this masterpiece of nature, this miracle of our days, must stay for ever on an island where no mortal man may dare approach her! But after all," he went on, "what does it matter that all the rest are banished, since I have the honour of being here, since I see her, hear her, admire her, since I love her better than my life!"

It was late, and the princess passed into a hall all of marble and porphyry, where fountains were playing, and everthing was pleasant and cool. As soon as she had entered, a symphony began and a sumptuous supper was served. At the side of the hall there were long aviaries filled with rare birds which Abricotine tended. Leander had learnt on his travels how to sing like birds; he used even to invent songs such as no living birds ever sang. The princess listened, looked in great astonishment, then left the table and came near. Ariel then gave out a louder, stronger note, and in the voice of a canary he sang these words to an impromptu air:

"O! heavy the tread of the march of life,
And weary the striving and vain the strife,

And lonely the way for you and for me
If Love be not of the company.
For life is love, and love is life,
And everything else is useless strife;
See, Love is beckoning you and me,
Haste then and join his company."

The princess, still more astonished, sent for Abricotine, and asked her if she had taught any of the canaries to sing. She said no, but she thought that canaries were probably as intelligent as parrots. The princess smiled, and thought all the same that Abricotine had given the birds singing lessons. Then she sat down to table again to finish her supper.

Leander's journey had been long enough to give him an appetite, and he made his way towards the good things, the very smell of which was grateful to him. The princess had a blue cat—a very fashionable colour for cats at that period—which she was very fond of, and one of her maidens held it in her arms, saying: "Madam, I assure you Bluet is hungry". So they seated him at the table, with a little golden plate and a lace napkin neatly folded. He wore a golden bell and a pearl collar. With a voracious appetite he began to eat. "Oh, ho!" said Ariel, "a great blue tom-cat, who probably never caught a mouse in his life, and who certainly is not of better birth than I, has the honour of supping with my fair princess! I would like to know if he loves her as much as I do, and if it is right that I have nothing but the smell of the dishes for my supper, while he munches all the dainty bits?" Thereupon he very quietly removed Bluet, sat down himself in the armchair, and took the cat on his lap. No one saw Ariel. How could they have seen him, for he had his little red hat on? The princess put partridge, quail, and pheasant on Bluet's golden plate. The partridge, quail, and pheasant disappeared in a moment, and the whole court said there never was a cat with such an appetite. The ragouts were excellent, too; and Ariel taking a fork, and holding it in the cat's paw, tasted them. Sometimes he took too much on his fork, and

Bluet, who did not understand a joke, mewed, and tried to scratch viciously. Then the princess would say: "Put that tart, or that fricassee, near poor Bluet. Hear how he is crying to have it!" Leander laughed to himself at such a funny adventure. But now he felt very thirsty, not being used to such long repasts without drinking. So he caught hold of a large melon with the cat's paw, and this satisfied him somewhat, and when supper was nearly over he ran to the sideboard and drank two bottles of delicious nectar.

The princess retired to her room, telling Abricotine to come along with her, and to shut the door. Ariel followed fast after, and made an unseen third to the company. The princess said to her confidante: "Confess, now, that you were exaggerating in drawing the portrait of this unknown prince. It does not seem to me possible for him to be so beautiful as you say." "I assure you, madam," she answered, "that if I have failed in any way it is that I have said too little." The princess sighed, and for a moment she was silent. Then, speaking again, she said: "It was wise of you to have refused to bring him with you." "But, madam," answered Abricotine, who was in fact a sly little monkey, and who already guessed what was in her mistress's mind, "even if he had come to admire the wonders of this lovely place, what harm could he have done you? Do you wish to live for ever unknown in a corner of the world, hidden away from the rest of mortals? What is the use of so much grandeur, pomp, and magnificence if nobody sees it all?" "Hold your tongue, you little chatterbox," said the princess, "and do not trouble the happy calm which has been mine for two hundred years. Think you, if I had lived an anxious, noisy life, I should have lived so long? It is only innocent and quiet pleasures that leave no bad effects behind. Have we not heard in the best histories of revolutions in great states, of the unforeseen strokes of fickle fortune, the terrible disturbances caused by love, the griefs of absence and of jealousy? What is it brings about all these sorrows and troubles? Nothing but the intercourse of human beings with each other. Now, thanks to the care of my mother, I am free from all these crosses. I know neither bitterness of heart, nor vain desires, nor envy, nor love, nor hate. Ah, let us go on living always in this same calm!" Abricotine dared not answer. The princess waited some time, and then asked her if she had nothing to say. Abricotine inquired why she had sent her portrait to various courts, where it could only make people miserable, for everyone who saw it would wish to see the original, and, being unable to, they would be in despair. "I confess, in spite of that," replied the princess, "that I would like my portrait to fall into the hands of that stranger, whose name I do not know." "Ah, madam!" she replied, "is he not already eager enough to see you? Would you have him more so?" "Yes," said the princess; "a certain impulse of vanity, which has been unknown to me till now, breeds this desire in me." Ariel listened to all this without losing a single one of the words: some of them gave him flattering hopes, which were dashed to pieces by others.

It grew late, and the princess went to her room to bed. Ariel would have much liked to have been present when she made her toilette, but though this was possible, the respect he had for her prevented him. It seemed to him that he ought to take no liberties with her but those she might have permitted; and his affection for her was so delicate and so refined that he tormented himself about the smallest things. So he went into a cabinet near the princess's room to have at least the pleasure of hearing her speak. At that moment she was asking Abricotine if she had seen nothing extraordinary during her little journey. "Madam," she said, "I passed through a forest where I saw animals very much like children. They were leaping and dancing about the trees like squirrels. They were very ugly, but wonderfully nimble." "Ah, how I should like to have some of them!" said the princess. "If they were less agile one could catch them." Ariel, who had passed through this forest, knew the animals must be monkeys. Thereupon he wished himself back in their haunts, where he caught a dozen, little and big. Putting them all into a sack, he wished

himself at Paris, where he had heard you could have anything you liked for money. So he went to Dautel, a dealer in curiosities, and bought a little golden coach, to which he harnessed six green monkeys, with little trappings of flame-coloured morocco pricked out with gold. Then he hastened to Johnson, a famous marionette showman, where he found two very clever monkeys—one, the more intelligent, called Joseph, the other Jonathan. They were very polite and very well-bred. Joseph he dressed as a king, and put him in the coach; Jonathan was the coachman, while the rest of the monkeys were pages. Never was seen anything so pretty. He put the carriage and the dressed-up monkeys in the same sack and returned. As the princess had not yet gone to bed she heard the noise of the little coach in her gallery, and her nymphs came to tell her of the arrival of the king of the dwarfs. At that moment the coach with its procession of monkeys entered her room, and the country monkeys did as pretty tricks as even Joseph and Jonathan. To tell the truth, it was Ariel who was leading the whole of them. Taking the monkey out of the little golden coach, he made him gracefully present a box covered with diamonds to the princess. She opened it at once, and found inside a letter, in which she read these verses:

"Here is pleasure's dwelling-place,
Palace bright, 'mid gardens shady;
Fair the spot and full of grace,
Yet not so fair as my fair lady.
All unseen, I envying see
Life's cool stream here calmly gliding;
Bound and struggling restlessly,
All my passion from her hiding."

It is not difficult to imagine her astonishment. Joseph made a sign to Jonathan to come and dance with him, and they excelled all the most celebrated performing monkeys that ever lived. But the princess, uneasy at being unable to guess whence the verses came, sent the dancers away sooner than she would otherwise have done, for they amused her endlessly, and she had laughed at first enough to make her ill. When they were gone she gave herself up entirely to her own thoughts, but she could make nothing of so dark a mystery.

Leander, much pleased by the interest with which his verses had been read, and by the delight of the princess in looking at the monkeys, now thought of taking some rest, of which he stood in much need. But he feared lest he might choose some room occupied by one of the princess's nymphs, and therefore he waited for a time in the great gallery of the palace. When at last he went downstairs, he found an open door, and entering noiselessly, found himself in a room on one of the lower floors—the prettiest, the pleasantest ever seen. The bed was hung with green and gold gauze, draped in festoons, with ropes of pearls and tassels of rubies and emeralds. It was still light enough to enable him to admire all this wonderful splendour. After shutting the door he fell asleep; but the remembrance of his fair princess woke him up several times, and he could not keep from heaving sighs for his great love for her.

He rose so very early that the time dragged till he could see her. Looking about him, he saw a canvas ready prepared, and colours, and he called to mind what his princess had said to Abricotine about her portrait. Now he could paint better than the great master, and without losing a moment he sat down before a large mirror and painted his own picture; also, in an oval, that of the princess, her face being so present to his imagination that he had no need to see her for this first sketch. Afterwards he touched up the work with her before him, though she was unconscious of his presence; and as it was the desire of pleasing her that gave him the impulse to work, never was a portrait more perfectly finished. He had represented himself as kneeling before her, holding the princess's portrait in one hand and in the other a scroll, on which was written:

"The likeness graven on my heart is fairer far."

When she entered the cabinet she was astonished to see there the portrait of a man, and she fixed her eyes on it with the greater wonder inasmuch as she recognised her own as well. The words written on the scroll gave her abundant matter for curiosity and thought. At that moment she was alone. She knew not what to think of such an extraordinary incident; but she persuaded herself it must be Abricotine who had played her this trick. The only thing to do was to find out whether the picture of this knight was painted from her imagination, or if there had been a living model. Getting up quickly, she ran to call Abricotine. Ariel was already in the cabinet with the little red hat, very curious to hear what would take place. The princess told Abricotine to cast her eyes on that picture, and tell her what she thought. As soon as she saw it she cried out: "Madam, I protest to you this is the portrait of that generous stranger to whom I owe my life. Yes, it is indeed the same; there is no doubt of it. These are his features, his figure, his hair, his whole bearing." "You pretend to be surprised," said the princess, smiling; "but it was you that put it here." "I, madam!" said Abricotine, "I swear to you I have never seen this picture before in all my life. Could I be so bold as to hide anything which could be of interest to you? And by what miracle could it have fallen into my hands? I cannot paint. No man has ever entered this place; yet—here he is, and painted along with you." "I am seized with terror," said the princess. "Some demon must have brought it here." "Madam," said Abricotine, "may it not have been Love? If you think so too, I advise you to have it burned at once." "What a pity that would be!" said the princess, sighing. "It seems to me my boudoir could have no prettier decoration than this picture." While she said so, she looked at it; but Abricotine persisted in saying she should burn a thing that could only have come there by magic power. "And these words—

'The likeness graven on my heart is fairer far,'"—

said the princess: "shall we burn them too?" "We must spare nothing," replied Abricotine, "not even your own portrait." She ran off at once to fetch a light. The princess went and stood near the window, unable to look any longer at a portrait which made such an impression on her heart. But Ariel, unwilling to let them burn it, took advantage of this moment, and ran off with it unseen.

Hardly was he out of the room when she turned round to look again at the magic portrait which pleased her so much. What was her surprise to see it gone! She looked on all sides. When Abricotine came in again the princess asked if it was she who had just taken it away, but Abricotine said "No," and this last adventure really did frighten them.

After hiding the portrait Leander came back. During these days it was a source of much delight to him to hear and see his fair princess. Every day he ate at the table along with the blue cat, whose appetite was none the more satisfied in consequence. Yet Ariel's happiness was far from perfect, since he dared neither speak nor let himself be seen, and without that one has little chance of being loved.

The princess delighted in all beautiful things, and in the present state of her heart she had need of amusement. One day when she was with her nymphs, she told them that she should like very much to know how the ladies of all the different courts in the universe were clad, in order that she might dress according to the finest model. A suggestion was all that Ariel wanted to make him set off on a journey through the whole earth. So, clapping on his little red hat, he wished himself in China, where he bought the finest stuffs and took patterns of the costumes. Then he flew to Siam, where he did the same. He ran through the four quarters of the world in three days, and when he was laden he came back to the Palace of Calm Delights, and hid in a room all that he had brought. When he had in this way collected a number of wonderful curiosities (for money was nothing to him, his rose furnishing

a constant supply), he bought five or six dozen dolls, which he had dressed in Paris, for there more than anywhere else in the world fashion has sway. There were costumes of all kinds, and of an untold splendour. All these Ariel arranged in the princess's cabinet.

When she entered she was surprised beyond words. Every doll carried a present, either watches, bracelets, diamond buttons, or necklaces, whilst the principal one had a case containing a portrait. Opening it, the princess found a miniature of Leander. Her remembrance of the first one made her recognise the second. She uttered a loud cry, then, looking at Abricotine, she said: "I cannot understand all that has been passing for some time in this palace. My birds talk like rational beings. It seems I have only to wish in order to be obeyed. I twice see the portrait of him who saved you from the bandits. Here are stuffs, diamonds, embroideries, lace, and wonderful curiosities. Who is then the fairy, who is the demon, that seeks with such care to please me so?" Leander, hearing her speak, wrote these words on his tablets, and threw them at the princess's feet:

"Neither sprite am I nor fairy;
But, though near you still I hover,
Yet to show my face I'm chary—
Pity your unhappy lover,
PRINCE ARIEL".

The tablets were so splendid with gold and jewels that as soon as she saw them she opened them, and read with the utmost astonishment what Leander had written. "This invisible creature must be a monster, then," she said, "since he dares not show himself; but if it were true that he had some attachment for me, he would surely have delicacy enough not to present me with so attractive a portrait. He cannot love me, else he would not expose my heart to this trial, or he has such a good opinion of himself that he thinks himself handsomer than he is in reality." "I have heard tell, madam," replied Abricotine, "that there are spirits made of air and fire; they have no body, and it is only their mind and their will that act." "I am very glad of it," replied the princess. "A lover like that could hardly disturb the calm of my life." Leander was delighted to hear her, and to see her so much occupied with his portrait. He called to mind that in a grotto which she often used to visit was a pedestal on which a Diana, still unfinished, was one day to be placed. He went and stood there in a strange dress, crowned with laurels and holding a lyre in his hand, which he could play better than Apollo. Then he waited patiently for his princess to come, as she did every day, for it was here she came to dream about her unknown lover. Abricotine's account of her champion, added to the pleasure she had in looking at Leander's picture, hardly left her a moment of rest. She loved solitude, and her merry humour had changed so much that her nymphs hardly recognised her.

When she entered the grotto, she signed to them not to follow her, so they each went away along separate walks. Meanwhile she threw herself on a grassy bed, sighing, shedding tears, even speaking, but so low that Ariel could not hear her. At first he had put on the little red hat, so that she might not see him. When he took it off she gazed on him with the utmost astonishment, imagining that it was a statue, for he tried not to change the attitude he had chosen. It was with a joy mingled with fear that she looked on him. This vision so unexpected filled her with surprise, but in the end the pleasure cast out the fear, and she was just growing used to seeing so lifelike a figure when the prince tuned his lyre and sang these words:

"There lurketh here such dangerous art
That sticks and stones might feel it.
In vain I vowed to guard my heart,
Nor let the fair ones steal it.
Now, wounded, who will heal it, will heal it?

"Is this the Isle of Calm Delights?
Here passion met me on the shore,
Made me a slave beneath his might;
Yet, spite of freedom heretofore,
'Tis here I'd stay for evermore, for evermore."

Although Leander's voice was charming, the princess could not master the terror that seized her. Suddenly she grew pale, and fell in a swoon. Ariel, alarmed, leaped from the pedestal to the ground, and put on his little red hat so that no one might see him. Then taking the princess in his arms, he tended her with the utmost care and eagerness. She opened her beautiful eyes and cast

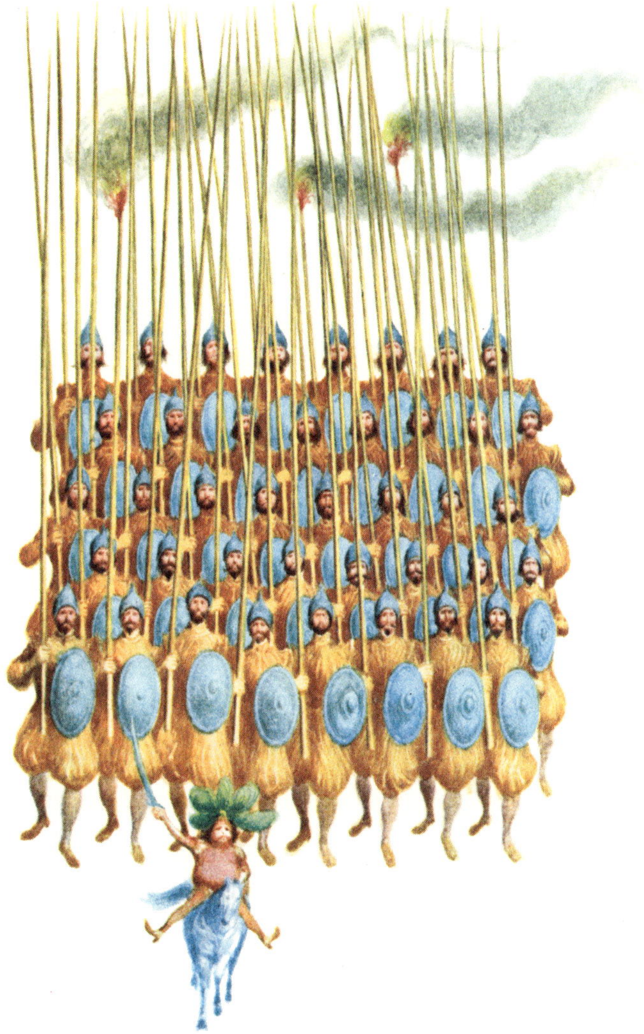

them about on all sides, as if to look for him. She saw no one, but yet she felt someone near her, holding her hands, kissing them, and moistening them with tears. It was long before she dared to speak, her flustered spirit hovering between fear and hope. She feared the invisible Ariel, but she loved him when he took the figure of the stranger. At last she cried out: "Ariel, brave Ariel, why are you not he whom I desire?" At these words Ariel was on the point of making himself known, but he dared not do it yet. "If I terrify this lady whom I love," he said, "if she fears me, she will never love me." This thought made him keep silence, and induced him to retire into a corner of the grotto. The princess, thinking she was alone, called for Abricotine, and told her the wonders of the animated statue, whose voice was so heavenly, and that in her swoon Ariel had tended her so well. "What a pity," she said, "that this spirit is deformed and hideous, for could anyone have more gracious and pleasant manners?" "And who told you," said Abricotine, "that he is as you imagine him to be? Did not Psyche think that love was a serpent? Your adventure is something like hers. You are no less beautiful. If it were Cupid that loved you, would you not love him?" "If Cupid and the unknown were the same," said the princess, blushing, "alas! I would indeed love Cupid. But how far I am from such happiness! I am following a chimera, and that fatal portrait of the stranger, added to what you have told me, makes me wish for things so opposed to my mother's precepts that I am sure to be punished." "Ah! Madam," said Abricotine, interrupting her, "have you not already trouble enough? Why look forward to the evils that will never come to pass?" It is easy to imagine all the pleasure such a conversation gave to Leander.

Meanwhile little Furibon, still in love with the princess, though he had never seen her, waited impatiently for the return of the four men whom he had sent to the Island of Calm Delights. Only one came back, who gave him an account of what had passed, telling him that it had been defended by Amazons, and

that unless he were to lead a great army there he would never enter the island. His father, the king, had just died, and Furibon now found himself sole master. So he gathered together more than four hundred thousand men, and set off at their head. Truly he was a fine general! Joseph or Jonathan would have done better than this dwarf, with his war-horse hardly half-an-ell in height. When the Amazons saw this great army they warned the princess, who at once sent Abricotine to the kingdom of the fairies to beg her mother to tell her what she should do to drive little Furibon out of her states. But Abricotine found the fairy very angry. "I know quite well all that my daughter is doing," she said. "Prince Leander is in her palace. He loves her, and she loves him. All my care has not been able to save her from the tyranny of love, and now she is under his fatal sway. Alas! the cruel god is not satisfied with the harm he has done me: he exercises his power on what I love better than my life. Such are the decrees of fate, and I cannot resist them. Return, Abricotine, I do not wish even to hear of the daughter who grieves me in this way."

Abricotine brought back the bad news to the princess, who was on the point of despair. Ariel was near her, invisible, and he saw with extreme sorrow her great grief. He did not dare to speak to her at that moment, but he remembered that Furibon was very avaricious, and that by giving him money he might be induced to go away. So he dressed himself as an Amazon, and wished himself first of all in the forest, that he might secure his horse. He called out: "Grisdelin!" and Grisdelin came to him, leaping and bounding, for he was very wearied at being so long away from his dear master. But when he saw him dressed as a woman he did not recognise him, and feared some mistake. When Leander arrived at Furibon's camp everybody took him for an Amazon, so handsome was he. The king was told that a young lady wished to deliver him a message from the Princess of Calm Delights, so, quickly putting on his royal robes, he went and sat on his throne, looking like a big toad playing at being king.

Leander spoke, telling him that the princess, who preferred a quiet, peaceful life to the troubles of war, sent to offer him as much money as he wanted if she might be left in peace; but that, if he refused her offer, she would take every means to defend herself. Furibon replied that he was willing to show mercy to her, that he accorded her the honour of his protection, and that she had only to send him a hundred thousand billions of pistoles and he would return at once to his own kingdom. Leander said it would take too long to count so many, but that he had only to say how many roomfuls he wished for, and that the princess was generous enough and rich enough not to look to a pistole more or less. Furibon was much astonished that instead of beating him down they proposed to give him even more than he demanded. He thought to himself that he would do well to take all the money he could get; then he could arrest the Amazon and kill her, so that she might not return to her mistress. So he told Leander he would like thirty very large rooms quite filled with gold pieces, and he would give his word as a king to go back to his own country. Leander was led into the rooms to be filled with gold, and, taking the rose, shook it and shook it till there rained from it torrents of pistoles, quadruples, louis, gold crowns, rose-nobles, sovereigns, guineas, sequins. Nothing could have been prettier than this shower of gold. Furibon was beside himself with joy, and the more gold he saw the more desirous was he of seizing the Amazon and carrying off the princess. As soon as the thirty rooms were full he cried to his guards: "Arrest that cheat!—it is false money she has brought me—arrest her." All the guards tried to get hold of the Amazon, but at that moment the little red hat was put on, and Ariel disappeared. They thought he had fled outside, and running after him, they left Furibon alone. Then Ariel took him by the hair, and cut off his head as if he had been a chicken, before ever the unfortunate little king could even see the hand that was taking his life.

As soon as Ariel had secured the king's head he wished himself

in the Palace of Delights. The princess was walking in the grounds, thinking in deep sadness of what her mother had said, and wondering what means she could take to repulse Furibon. It was a very difficult task for her and her little band of Amazons, who could not possibly defend her against four hundred thousand men. All at once she saw a head in the air, no one holding it, which astonished her so much that she did not know what to think. It was much worse when the head was placed at her feet by some unseen hand. Then she heard a voice saying: "Fear no more, dear princess; Furibon will never again do you wrong." Abricotine recognised the voice of Leander, and cried out: "I assure you, madam, that the unseen one who is speaking is the stranger who

came to my aid." The princess was astonished and delighted. "Ah!" she said, "if it is true that Ariel and the stranger are the same, I confess I should be very pleased to prove my gratitude to him." Ariel went away, saying: "I want still to work that I may be worthy of her". And he returned to the army of Furibon, the noise of whose death had been spread abroad. As soon as he appeared amongst them in his ordinary dress, everyone came up to him: the captains and the soldiers surrounded him, shouting aloud for joy, proclaiming him their king, and telling him the crown belonged to him. He divided the thirty rooms full of gold generously amongst them, so that the soldiers were made rich for ever. And after some formalities, which assured Leander of the loyalty of the soldiers, he returned to the princess, ordering his army to make their way gradually back to his own kingdom.

The princess had gone to bed when Leander returned to the palace, and the deep respect which he had for her prevented his entering her room. So he went to his own, for he still kept the one below. He was tired enough to be glad of some rest, and this made him forget to shut the door as carefully as he usually did. The princess, who was in a fever of anxiety, got up before the dawn, and in her morning-gown went to her room downstairs. But what was her surprise to find Leander asleep on a bed! She had time enough to look at him without being seen, and to be convinced that it was the person whose portrait was in the diamond case. "It is not possible," she said, "that it is Ariel; for, do spirits sleep? Is that body made of air or fire, as Abricotine said? Does it not fill space?" She touched his hair gently: she heard him breathe, and she could not tear herself away, being half delighted and half alarmed at having found him. Just as she was looking at him with eager eyes, her fairy mother entered with such a terrible noise that Leander awoke with a start. How surprised, how grieved he was to see his princess in the utmost despair! Her mother was dragging her off, loading her with reproaches. Oh, what grief for these young lovers about to be separated for ever! The princess dared not say a word

to this terrible fairy, and turned her eyes towards Leander as if to ask for help. He knew well enough that he could not keep her against the wish of so powerful a lady; but he trusted somewhat to his persuasive tongue and the mildness of his manner for appeasing this angry mother. He ran after her, threw himself at her feet, and begged her to take pity on a young king who would never cease to love her daughter, and whose highest happiness would be to make her happy. The princess, encouraged by his example, then clung about her mother's knees, saying that without the king she could not be content, and she owed him much. "You do not know the trouble of love," cried the fairy, "nor the treasons of which lovers are capable. They only fascinate in order to poison us. I have experienced it. Do you wish your fate to be like mine?" "Ah, madam," replied the princess, "is there no exception? Do you not think that the assurances which the king gives you, and which seem so sincere, will shelter me from what you dread?"

But the obstinate fairy let them sigh at her feet. In vain did they moisten her hands with their tears. She took no notice, and she would certainly never have forgiven them had not the lovely Fairy Gentille appeared in the room, shining brighter than the sun. The Graces accompanied her, and she was followed by a troop of loves, of sports, and of pleasures, who sang a thousand pretty songs that had never been heard before, dancing about as merry as children the while. Embracing the old fairy, Gentille said: "My dear sister, I am sure you have not forgotten the services I did you when you wished to return to our kingdom. Had it not been for me you would never have been received. Since then I have asked for nothing in return; but at last the time is come when you can do me a real favour. Forgive this fair princess; give your consent to her marriage with this young king, and I will answer for him that he will never cease to love her. The web of their life will be spun with threads of silk and gold, and their union will give you infinite pleasure, while I shall never forget the kindness you have done me." "I consent to all you ask, dear Gentille," cried the fairy.

"Come, my children, come to my arms, and receive the assurance of my love." With that she embraced the princess and her lover. The Fairy Gentille was full of joy, and the whole troop began to sing the wedding hymns; and the soft music having awakened all the nymphs of the palace, they came running in their light gauze robes to learn what was happening. Here was a pleasant surprise for Abricotine! No sooner had she set eyes on Leander than she recognised him; and seeing him holding the princess's hand, she felt sure that they had both been made happy. What confirmed her was that the fairy mother said she would transport the Isle of Calm Delights, with the castle and all the wonders it contained, into Leander's kingdom; that she would dwell with them there, and would heap still greater riches on them. "Whatever your generosity may suggest to you to bestow on me," answered the king, "it is impossible that you can give me anything equal to what I have received to-day." This little compliment pleased the fairy very much, for she belonged to the olden time, when they would compliment each other all day long for some trifle no bigger than a pin-point.

As Gentille had forgotten nothing, she had had the generals and the captains of Furibon's army brought to the palace of the princess, in order that they might be present at the splendid feast that was about to take place. It was she who took charge of the arrangements; and five or six volumes would not be enough to describe the comedies, the operas, the running at the ring, the music, the gladiator fights, the hunts, and the other splendid amusements of this charming wedding-feast. But, most wonderful of all, each nymph found, among the brave soldiers that Gentille had brought to this beautiful spot, a husband as affectionate as if she had known him for ten years. Yet their acquaintance had only lasted four-and-twenty hours; but then the little wand can do even more wonderful things than that.

ONCE upon a time there lived a king and a queen who had two fine boys. They grew like the day, and were hungry and healthy. The queen never had any children born to her without sending for the fairies to ask what would be their future lot. So at the birth of her next child, a pretty little girl—so pretty that you could not look on her without loving her—the queen entertained in a very hospitable fashion all the fairies who came to see her on the occasion. As they were going away, she said to them: "Do not forget that good custom of yours; and tell me what will happen to Rosette." (Rosette was the little princess's name.) The fairies said they had left their fortune-books at home, and that they would come back again to see her. "Ah!" said the queen, "that bodes nothing good. You do not want to distress me by foretelling evil, but let me know all, I beg of you, and hide nothing from me." They excused themselves in all kinds of ways, but this only made the queen more anxious to know what was in their minds. At last, the chief fairy said: "Madam, we fear that Rosette may be a source of great misfortune to her brothers, and that they may die on her account. That is all we can find out about the fate of this pretty little girl, and we are very sorry not to be able to tell you anything more cheerful." They went away, and the queen was so very, very downcast that the king saw it from her face. He asked her what was the matter, and she told him she had gone too near the fire and had burnt all the flax on her distaff. "Is that all?" said the king. And he went up to the garret and brought her more flax than she could spin in a hundred years.

But still the queen was sad, and he asked her again what was the matter. She told him that when she was standing on the edge of the river, she had let her green satin slipper fall in. "Is that all?" said the king. And he sent for all the shoemakers in his kingdom, and bought her ten thousand green satin slippers.

But still the queen was sad, and again he asked her what was the matter. She told him that while eating very heartily, she had swallowed the wedding-ring on her finger. The king knew she was not telling the truth, for he had put the ring away carefully; so he said to her: "My dear wife, you are not speaking the truth. Here is your ring, which I put away in my purse." Now she was caught in the very act of telling a lie, and there is nothing in the world uglier. She saw that the king was offended, so she told him what the fairies had predicted about little Rosette, and asked him, if he knew any good remedy, to tell her of it. The king was very down-hearted; so much so, that at last he said to the queen: "I know no other way of saving our two sons but of killing the little girl before she is out of her swaddling clothes." But the queen cried out that she would rather die herself than consent to such a cruel deed, and that he must think of some other means.

During this time, when they could think of nothing else, the queen learnt that in a large wood near the town there lived an old hermit, who was consulted by persons far and near. "I must go to him also," she said. "The fairies told me the evil, but they forgot to tell me the cure." So early one morning she set out on a pretty little white mule shod with gold, two of her maids accompanying her, each on a beautiful horse. When they came near the wood the queen and her maidens dismounted out of respect, and took their way to the tree where the hermit dwelt. He did not much care for visits from women folk, but when he saw that it was the queen, he said: "Welcome! What can I do for you?" Then, telling him what the fairies had said of Rosette, she asked his advice; and he told her she must shut the princess up in a tower, and never let her out. The queen thanked him, made him a handsome present, and came back to tell the king everything.

When the king heard the news he had a great tower built

without delay, and there he locked up his daughter. So that she might not be lonely, the king, the queen, and her two brothers went to see her every day. The elder brother was called the big prince, and the younger the little prince. They loved their sister passionately, for she was the prettiest and the most graceful little girl that ever was seen, and a glance from her eye was better to them than a hundred pounds. When she was fifteen years old, the big prince said to the king: "Father, my sister is old enough now to be married. Shall we not soon dance at her wedding?" And the little prince said the same thing to the queen; and their majesties joked with them, but gave them no answer about the marriage. At

last the king and queen fell very ill, and died almost on the same day. Everybody mourned very deeply, and put on black clothes, and all the death-bells were rung. Rosette was inconsolable for the death of her good mother. When the funeral of the king and queen was over, the marquises and the dukes of the kingdom led the elder prince to a throne made of gold and diamonds, and seated him on it. He had a beautiful crown on his head, and his garments were of violet velvet, covered with suns and moons. Then all the court shouted thrice: "Long live the king!" And there was nothing heard but sounds of joy.

The king and his brother in the meanwhile said to each other: "Now that we are masters, we must release our sister from the tower, where for long she has been pining." They had only to cross the garden to reach the tower, which was built in a corner, as high as the builders could make it, for the late king and queen had wished her to stay there always. Rosette, who was embroidering a beautiful gown on a frame in front of her, rose on seeing her brothers, and taking the king's hand she said: "Good-day, your majesty; you are now king, and I am your little servant. I beg that you will release me from the tower, where I am so very lonely," and with that she began to cry. The king kissed her, and told her not to cry: for he had come to take her away to a beautiful castle. The prince had his pockets full of sugar-plums, and these he gave to Rosette. "Come along," he said, "let us get out of this hideous tower. The king will soon have you married, so don't distress yourself."

When Rosette saw the beautiful garden full of flowers, and fruit, and fountains, she was so astonished that she could not say a word; for till this day she had seen nothing. She looked all round on every side, walked on for a little way, then stopped to pick fruit from the trees, or flowers from the flower-beds. Her little one-eared dog, Fretillon, as green as a parrot, and an exquisite dancer, ran before her, saying yap, yap, yap, and jumping and capering madly. Fretillon amused the company very much. Suddenly he set

off at a run into a little wood. The princess followed him, and great was her astonishment when she saw a huge peacock spreading out its tail; it seemed to her so very, very beautiful that she could not take her eyes off it. The king and the prince coming up wished to know what was amusing her. She pointed to the peacock, and asked what it was. They told her it was a bird which sometimes was eaten. "What!" she said. "Do they dare to kill such a beautiful bird and eat it? I declare that I shall never marry anyone but the King of the Peacocks, and when I am their queen I shall let nobody eat them." The astonishment of the king is not to be told. "But, my sister," he said, "where think you we shall find this King of the Peacocks?" "Wherever you like, your majesty; but I will marry none but him."

After this decision, the two brothers took her to their castle, where the peacock had to be brought, and kept in her room, so fond was she of it. All the court ladies who had not yet seen Rosette hastened to salute her, and to pay their respects to her, some bringing her preserves, some sugar, others dresses trimmed with gold, others beautiful ribbons, dolls, embroidered shoes, pearls, and diamonds. Everywhere they did honour to her; and she was so well-bred, so polite, kissing their hands, and bowing when anything pretty was given her, that there was not a gentleman or a lady of the court who did not go away satisfied.

While she was in this good company the king and the prince were thinking over what means they would take to find the King of the Peacocks, if there was such a person in the world. They thought it would be necessary to have a portrait of Princess Rosette painted, so they had this done. It was so like, that only speech was lacking. Then they said to her: "Since you will marry none but the King of the Peacocks, we are going away together to seek him for you through the whole world. If we find him we shall be very glad. Take care of our kingdom till we return."

Rosette thanked them for the trouble they were taking for her, and promised to govern their kingdom well. While they were away, she said, her whole amusement would be in looking at the beautiful peacock, and in making Fretillon dance. They could not help weeping when they said good-bye.

So the two princes set off, asking everyone they met on their way if they did not know the King of the Peacocks. But everyone said: "No, we do not know him." They passed on and went still further, and such a long, long way did they travel that they reached where no one had ever been before. They came at last to the kingdom of the mayflies. Never were so many seen before, and they made such a loud buzzing that the king was afraid lest he should become deaf. He asked the one that appeared the most sensible if he knew where he could find the King of the Peacocks. "Sire," said the mayfly, "his kingdom is thirty thousand leagues from here. You have taken the longest way to reach it." "And how do you know that?" said the king. "Because," replied the mayfly, "we know you very well, and every year we spend two or three months in your gardens." Then the king and his brother saluted the mayfly in the most affectionate manner, and struck up a great friendship with him. They dined together, and went to look with the greatest admiration at all the curiosities of that country, where the tiniest leaf of a tree is worth a pound. After that they went on their journey again, and as they now knew the way they were not long before they arrived. All the trees they saw laden with peacocks, and the whole place was so full of them that you could hear their cries and chattering two leagues off.

The king said to his brother: "If the King of the Peacocks is himself a peacock, how can our sister ever marry him? We should be mad if we gave our consent. Think what a fine connection she would give us. Why, we should have little peacocks for nephews!" And the prince was no less troubled. "Yes," he said; "it is indeed a most unfortunate idea that she has taken into her head. I can't think how she has thought of the existence even of a peacock king."

When they reached the great town they saw it was full of men and women, but their clothes were made of peacocks' feathers, and these were everywhere about as if much prized for their beauty. They met the king driving in a pretty little coach of gold and diamonds, drawn by twelve peacocks at full gallop. The king was so very beautiful that the stranger king and the prince were charmed. He had long, flaxen, curly hair, a fair complexion, and a peacock's tail for a crown. When he saw them he thought, since their dress was different from that of the people of the country, they must be foreigners, and to find out he stopped his coach and called them towards him.

The king and the prince came forward. Having made a low bow, they said: "Your majesty, we come from a long distance to show you a beautiful portrait," and they drew from their valise the large picture of Rosette. When the King of the Peacocks had looked well at it, he said: "I cannot believe that there is so beautiful a maiden in the whole world." "She is a hundred times more beautiful than that," said the king. "Ah," said the Peacock King; "you are laughing at me." "Sire," said the prince, "this is my brother, a king like yourself. That is his title, and I am called the prince. Our sister, whose portrait you see, is the Princess Rosette. We come to ask you if you will marry her. She is beautiful and very good, and we shall give her a bushel of gold." "Ah, but with all my heart!" said the king. "With me she shall lack for nothing. I will love her dearly. But I assure you I demand that she be as beautiful as her portrait, and if she fails in the slightest degree in her resemblance to it, I shall put you to death." "Very well, we agree," said Rosette's two brothers. "You agree?" said the king. "Then go to prison and stay there till the princess arrives." The princes made no objection, for they were very certain that Rosette was more beautiful than her portrait.

While they were in prison, the king had everything possible done for their comfort, and he went himself to see them very often. In his castle he kept Rosette's portrait, with which he was so infatuated that he never slept day or night. As soon as the king and his brother were in prison, they sent word by post to the princess to pack up quickly, and to come without delay, for at last the Peacock King was waiting for her. But they said nothing about their being prisoners, for fear she should be too anxious. When she received this letter she was so overwhelmed with joy that she was like to die. She told everybody that the Peacock King was found and wanted to marry her. They lit bonfires, and fired cannon, and ate sweetmeats and sugar-plums to their hearts' content, and all those who came to see the princess for three days had bread and jam, and wafers and chocolates given them. After having dispensed these

bounties she left her beautiful dolls to her good friends, and gave her brother's kingdom into the keeping of the wisest old men of the town, charging them to take good care of everything, to spend little, and to save up money against the return of the king. She left her peacock behind in her friends' keeping, only taking with her her nurse and her foster-sister, and her little green dog Fretillon. Then she set out in a boat on the sea, taking with her the bushel of golden crowns, and dresses to last her for ten years even were she to change them twice a day. She and her companions did nothing but laugh and sing. The nurse asked the boatman: "Are we near, are we anywhere near the kingdom of the peacocks?" He answered: "No." And again this time she asked: "And now, are we near it, anywhere near it?" And he answered: "Soon, we shall soon be there." Still another time she said: "Are we near, are we anywhere near it?" "Yes, yes, we are," he answered. And when he had said that she went to the end of the boat, sat down beside him, and said: "If you wish it, you can be rich for ever." "Very well," he answered. "If you like, you can earn good money." "I have no objections," he said. "Well, then, this night while the princess is asleep you must help me to throw her into the water. After she is drowned I shall dress my daughter up in her fine clothes, and we shall take her to the Peacock King, who will be very glad to marry her. For your reward we shall give you as many diamonds as you like." The boatman was much astonished at the nurse's proposal. He said it was a pity to drown so beautiful a princess, and that he was sorry for her. But she took a bottle of wine and made him drink so much that he was not in a condition to refuse her.

Night having come, the princess went to bed as usual, her little Fretillon snugly rolled up at her feet. Rosette was fast asleep when the wicked nurse, who was very wide awake, went to fetch the boatman. She took him to the princess's room, and then without awaking her, they took her, feather-bed, mattress, sheets, coverlet, and all, her foster-sister helping them in every way, and threw her with all these into the sea. And the princess slept so soundly that she did not awake. But most fortunately her bed was made of phoenixes' feathers, which are very rare, and which have this property, that they never go to the bottom of the water. So that she floated about in her bed, as if she had been in a boat. The water, however, gradually wet first her feather-bed and then her mattress, through, and Rosette, beginning to feel the discomfort of this, was turning from one side to the other when Fretillon woke up. His scent was keen, and he smelt the soles and the cod-fish so near that he began to bark loud enough to wake up the other fishes. They began to swim about, the big ones pushing against the princess's bed which, being unattached, turned round and round and round about. Oh, how astonished she was! "Is our boat dancing on the water?" she said. "I am not used to being so uncomfortable as I am to-night." And Fretillon went on barking, barking, in the most desperate fashion. Meanwhile the wicked nurse and the boatman, who were listening from far off, said: "There is that funny little dog and his mistress drinking our healths. Make haste to reach the shore." For they were now opposite the town of the Peacock King.

He had sent to the sea coast a hundred carriages, drawn by all sorts of strange animals—lions, bears, deer, wolves, horses, oxen, asses, eagles, and peacocks, and to the carriage for the Princess Rosette were harnessed six blue monkeys that could jump, and dance on tight ropes, and do all sorts of funny tricks. They had beautiful harnesses of crimson velvet with golden mountings. Sixty young damsels appeared, chosen by the king to amuse Rosette. They were dressed in all kinds of colours, and lavishly adorned with gold and silver.

The nurse had taken great care to dress her daughter gaily, putting Rosette's diamonds on her head and all over her, and giving her her prettiest gown. But, with all her ornaments, she was uglier than an ape. Her hair was of a greasy black, her eyes squinting, her legs twisted, and she had a great hump in the middle of her back. Besides, she was ill-tempered and sulky, and always grumbling.

When the Peacock King's people saw her come out of the boat, they were so very much surprised that they could not say a word. "What is the matter?" she said. "Are you asleep? Quick, make haste, bring me something to eat! You rascals, I shall have you all hung!" When they heard this they said: "What a hideous creature! And she is as wicked as she is ugly! This is a fine marriage our king is making! Well, we are not astonished! But it was hardly worth while to bring her from the other end of the world." Meanwhile she was carrying things with a high hand, and for no reason at all she was boxing people's ears and hitting them with her fist. As her procession was very long, she went slowly, sitting up proudly like a queen in her carriage. All the peacocks perched themselves on the trees to salute her as she passed, meaning to shout "Long live the fair Queen Rosette!" but when they saw her looking so hideous, they called out: "Fie, fie! how ugly she is!" She was mad with rage, and screamed to her guards: "Kill those rascally peacocks that are shouting insults at me." The peacocks flew away fast enough, laughing at her. The wicked boatman, who saw what was going on, said to the nurse under his breath: "Mother, we don't seem to be getting on very well. It is a pity your daughter is not prettier." But she whispered: "Hold your tongue, you fool, else you will spoil everything."

The king was told by this time that the princess was coming. "Well, now," said he, "did her brothers tell the truth? Is she more beautiful than her portrait?" "She will do very well, your majesty," said those to whom he spoke, "if she is as beautiful." "Oh, yes," said the king; "I shall be satisfied. Let us now go and see her," for he heard by the great noise they were making in the court-yard that she had arrived. The only words he could distinguish out of all they were saying were: "Yes, how ugly she is!" He thought they must be speaking of some dwarf or of some beast she had perhaps brought with her, for it did not even enter his mind that it could really be herself.

Rosette's portrait, uncovered, was carried at the end of a long pole, and the king walked gravely behind, with all his barons and all his peacocks, and then all the ambassadors from the neighbouring kingdoms. The king was full of impatience to see his dear Rosette. Oh! when he did see her—he all but died on the spot. He flew into the greatest passion, tore his clothes, and refused to go near her, for she terrified him.

"What!" he said. "Those two villains I have in my prison have been bold enough to laugh at me, and to propose a monkey like that for my wife? They shall die! Go, let the guards without a moment's delay shut up that insolent woman, her nurse, and the man who brought them here, and cast them into the dungeon of my great tower."

Meanwhile the king and his brother, who were prisoners, and who knew that their sister was about to arrive, had put on their best clothes to meet her. But instead of coming to open the prison and setting them free as they had hoped, the gaoler came with the soldiers and took them down to a cellar which was quite dark and full of hideous beasts, and where they stood in water up to their necks. No one could have been more astonished or distressed than were they. "Alas!" they said to each other; "this is a sad wedding for us. What can have brought so great a misfortune on us?" They did not know what in the world to think, except that the king meant to put them to death, and right sorrowful they were.

Three days passed and they had no explanation given them. At the end of that time the Peacock King came to the prison and said the most insulting things to them through a hole. "You have taken the title of king and prince to catch me and to persuade me to marry your sister. But you are rascals, both of you, not worth the water you drink. I shall bring you before the judges, who will settle your case fast enough, and already the rope to hang you with is being made." "King of the Peacocks," answered the other king, angrily, "do not be so hasty in this matter, or you may repent of it. I am as much a king as you. I have a great kingdom. I am rich in suits and crowns, and have broad gold pieces in plenty. Surely you must be joking to talk of hanging us. Have we stolen anything from you?"

When the king heard him speak so boldly he did not know what to think, and he had half a mind to let them go with their sister without putting them to death, but his chief friend, who was a mere flatterer, encouraged him, telling him that if he did not revenge himself everybody would laugh at him, and would take him for a miserable little king not worth a penny. So he swore he would not pardon them, and he ordered them to be tried. The trial did not last long, for to look at the portrait of the Princess Rosette beside the pretender that had come in her place was quite enough. So they were condemned to be beheaded, as liars who had promised the king a beautiful princess, and had given him instead an ugly peasant girl. Then the judge went to the prison with much ceremony to declare the sentence. The prisoners said they had not lied, that their sister was indeed a princess, that she was fairer than the day, and that there was something behind all this that they did not understand, and that if but seven days' grace were given them before being put to death, perchance in that time their innocence would be recognised. It was hard to persuade the King of the Peacocks, who was very angry, to grant them this grace, but at last he consented.

While all these things were passing at the court, we must tell something about poor Princess Rosette. As soon as it was day she was much astonished, and so was Fretillon, at seeing herself in the middle of the sea, with no boat and utterly helpless. Then she began to cry and cry till all the fish were sorry for her. She did not know what to do, nor what would become of her. "Surely," said she, "I have been thrown into the sea by order of the Peacock King. He has repented of marrying me, and to get rid of me without disgrace to himself he has had me drowned. What a strange man!" she went on. "I should so have loved him, and we should have been the happiest of couples." Thereupon she wept very bitterly, for she could not help loving him. Two days she remained in this condition, floating from one end of the sea to the other, wet to her very bones, chilled to death, and almost benumbed. If it had not been for little Fretillon, who warmed her heart a little, she would have died a hundred times. She was famished with hunger, and seeing oysters, she took as many as she wanted and ate them. Fretillon did not much like them, but he had nothing else to eat. When night came on a great fear took possession of Rosette, and she said to her dog: "Fretillon, keep on barking, for fear the soles eat us up." He had barked the whole night long, and the princess's bed was not far from the sea-shore. Near them there was a good old man, who lived quite alone in a little hut where nobody ever went. He was very poor, and had no longings for the goods of this world. When he heard Fretillon barking, he was very much astonished, for it was very rarely that dogs passed by there. He thought some travellers must have lost their way, and he went out with the kind intention of putting them on their road again. All at once he saw the princess and Fretillon floating in the sea. The princess at sight of him held out her arms, crying: "Good old man, save me, for I shall perish here. For two days I have been in this condition." When he heard her speaking in this sad voice, he felt great pity for her, and returned to his hut again to fetch a large hook. The water reached to his neck as he went in, and two or three times he thought he should be drowned. At last with tremendous efforts he brought the bed to the shore. Rosette and Fretillon were very glad to be on dry land again, and thanked the good man with much gratitude. Then she took the coverlet in which she was wrapped, and barefooted she entered the hut, where he lit her a little fire of dry straw, and took out of his trunk his late wife's best dress and shoes and stockings, which the princess put on. Clad thus like a peasant, she looked as beautiful as the day, and Fretillon danced round her to amuse her.

The old man saw well enough that Rosette was some great lady, for the covers of her bed were all of gold and silver, and her mattress was of satin. He begged her to tell him her story, promising not to repeat a word if she did not wish him to. She told him everything from one end to the other, weeping very bitterly, for she still believed that it was the King of the Peacocks that had ordered her to be drowned. "How shall we manage, my daughter?" said the old man. "You are such a great princess and used to eating only dainty morsels, and I have only black bread and radishes. It will be but poor cheer for you. If you will but let me, I shall go and tell the Peacock King that you are here; for of a surety, had he seen you, he would marry you." "Ah, he is a wicked man; he would kill me. But if you have a little basket fasten it round my dog's neck, and he will not have his usual luck if he does not bring us back something to eat." The old man gave the princess a basket, which she tied round Fretillon's neck, saying: "Run off to the place where the best dinner in the whole town is being cooked and bring it back to me." Fretillon ran to the town; and as there was no better pot than the king's, he went into the royal kitchen, found the pot, took very cunningly all that was in it, and returned home. Then Rosette said to him: "Run back again to the larder and take the best of everything there." Fretillon flew back to the larder, carried off white bread, muscatel wine, all kinds of fruits and preserves, and he was so laden that he was quite exhausted.

When the Peacock King wished to dine, there was nothing in his pot nor in his larder. Each one of his servants looked at the other, and the king was in a terrible rage. "Well," said he, "I cannot dine, but this evening let the spit be put on the fire so that I may have good roast meat." The evening being come, the princess said to Fretillon: "Run off to the town, go to the best kitchen, and bring me some good roast meat." Fretillon did as his mistress bade him, and knowing of no better kitchen than the king's, he went in very quietly, while the cooks' backs were turned, and took the whole roast on the spit. It looked delicious, and the very sight of it would have made you hungry. He brought back his basketful to the princess, who sent him back again to the larder to bring all kinds of sweets and sugar-plums. The king, who had had no dinner, wished to sup early, but there was nothing for him. He flew into a fearful rage, and went to bed without supper. Next day at dinner and supper the same thing happened, so that the king was three days without eating or drinking; for whenever he sat down to table, it was found that everything had been stolen. His confidant, in great trouble, and fearing the king would die, hid himself in a little corner of the kitchen, and kept his eyes on the boiling pot. How astonished he was to see a little green dog, with but one ear, creep in softly, lift the lid of the pot, and put the meat in its basket. Following it to know where it would go, he saw it run outside the town, and following it still farther, he found himself at the good old man's house. Without delay he went and told the king that it was to a poor peasant's hut that his boil and roast went every evening and morning.

The king was much astonished, and ordered them to go and make inquiries. The confidant, anxious for the king's favour, went himself, taking a guard of archers with him. They found the peasant dining with the princess and eating the king's boiled beef. They were both seized and bound with stout cords, and Fretillon was captured as well. When they had arrived at the palace the king was told. "To-morrow," said he, "is the last of the seven days

I gave the wicked men to live. They shall die with those who stole my dinner." Then he strode into the justice chamber. The old man fell on his knees saying he would explain everything. But while he was speaking the king looked on the beautiful princess, and was sorry to see her weep. Then when the good man had declared that she was called Rosette, and that they had thrown her into the sea, in spite of his weakness from his long fast the king gave three leaps for joy, embraced her, and untied the cords with which she was bound, telling her he loved her with all his heart. At once the princes were fetched, but they, thinking it was to take them to their deaths, came out very sad and hanging their heads. The nurse and her daughter were brought too. When they were face to face they all knew each other. Rosette fell on her brothers' necks; the nurse and her daughter and the boatman fell on their knees, and asked for pardon. The joy was so great that the king and the princess forgave the evil-doers; and the good old man received a large reward, and stayed for the rest of his life in the palace.

In the end, the Peacock King made every possible amends to the other king and his brother, to show his grief for having treated them so badly; and the nurse gave Rosette back her fine dresses and her bushel of gold. The wedding-feast lasted for fifteen days. Everyone was full of joy; even Fretillon had his share, for he ate nothing but partridge meat for the rest of his life.

The Golden Branch

THERE was once a king whose temper was so austere and morose that all who knew him feared rather than loved him. Very rarely did he show himself; and on the slightest suspicion he would put his subjects to death. And because he was always frowning they called him King Sombre. Now King Sombre had a son who was not in the least like him. There was no other prince in the world so clever, or so gentle, or so generous, or of such various talents. But his legs were crooked; he had a hump higher than his head; his eyes squinted, and his mouth was awry. In short, he was a little monstrosity, and never was so fair a soul the light of so hideous a body. Yet by some strange chance he made himself beloved by all whom he cared to please; and in intelligence he was so much superior to anyone else that no one could hear him talk without being interested. The queen, his mother, wished to call him Torticoli, either because she liked the name, or because, on account of his crookedness, she thought she had hit on the aptest name possible. King Sombre, who thought more of his own greatness than the happiness of his son, cast his eyes on the daughter of a powerful king, one of his neighbours, whose states, if added to his own, would make him formidable throughout the earth. He thought this princess a most fitting match for Prince Torticoli, inasmuch as she would never be able to reproach him for his ugliness, being herself at least as ugly and deformed as he was. She used always to go about in a litter, for her legs were weak. Her name was Trognon. For all her defects she was the most lovable creature in the world, and it seemed as if heaven had wished to give her compensation for the wrong that nature had done her.

King Sombre asked for and obtained the picture of the Princess Trognon, and placed it in a great hall under a canopy. Then he sent for Prince Torticoli, and commanded him to look on the portrait with favour, since it was Trognon's, and she was to be his wife. Torticoli glanced at it, and then turned away his eyes with a scornful air that displeased his father. "Are you not satisfied?" he asked, in a bitter, angry tone. "No, sire," he answered. "I should never be satisfied to marry a person like her." "It is indeed most fitting for you to point out the faults in this princess," said King Sombre, "a hideous little monster like you, whose very look frightens people." "That is the very reason," said the prince, "why I do not wish to wed with just such another monster. It is enough to have to endure the sight of myself. What would it be were there a whole tribe of us?" "You are afraid lest the race of monsters be perpetuated?" said the king, in an angry tone. "Well, your fears are of no avail, for you shall marry her. It is enough that I command. It is your part to obey." Torticoli answered nothing, but with a deep bow he left the hall.

King Sombre was not accustomed to the slightest resistance to his wishes, and his son's put him into a fearful temper. So he shut him up in a tower built expressly for rebel princes. But there had been none there for two hundred years, so everything about it was in very bad repair, and all the rooms and the furniture seemed to be very old. The prince, who was very fond of reading, asked for books, so they let him take some from the library in the tower. At first he thought that this permission was all that was necessary, but when he tried to read them he found they were in a tongue so ancient that he did not understand a word of it. He put them aside, but afterwards he took them up again, trying to make out something of their contents, or at least to amuse himself. King Sombre, feeling sure that Torticoli would get tired of prison, acted as if the prince had given his consent to marry Trognon, and sent ambassadors to the neighbouring king asking for the hand of his daughter, to whom he promised perfect happiness. Trognon's father was delighted to find such a good chance of marrying her, for it was not everybody who would be willing to take on himself the care of the ugly creature. So he accepted King Sombre's proposal, though, to tell the truth, the portrait of Torticoli, which they had brought, did not strike him as very attractive. It also was placed in a magnificent gallery, and Trognon was sent for. As soon as she saw it she lowered her eyes and began to cry. Her father, very angry at the evident dislike she showed, took a mirror, and placing it in front of her, said: "You weep, my daughter? Well, look at yourself, and be convinced after that that you have nothing to weep for." "If I were in any hurry to get married, sire," she answered, "I should perhaps be to blame for my fastidiousness; but I would rather bear my troubles all alone. I do not wish to share with anyone the misery of looking on my face. Let me remain my whole life long unhappy Princess Trognon. I shall be content—at least I shall make no complaint." No matter how reasonable were her words, the king would not listen to them, and she had to go with the ambassadors who had come for her.

While she is travelling in a litter, let us go back to the tower and see what the prince is doing. None of his keepers dared speak to him, for they had been told to wear him out, to give him bad food, and to exhaust his patience by every kind of cruel treatment. And King Sombre knew how to make people obey him—if not from love, then from fear. But the guards' affection for the prince was very great, and they found means to ease some part of his sufferings. One day when he was walking in a large gallery, thinking sadly of the unhappy lot which had made him so ugly, so unsightly, and which had thrown in his way a princess still more so, he cast his eyes on the windows, which were painted in very bright colours and fine designs. Having a great love for such works of art, he set about examining this one. But he could not understand the subject, for it dealt with things gone by ages since. But one figure particularly struck him—a man so like himself that it might have been his own portrait. This man was in the dungeon

of the keep searching for something in the wall. There he found a golden screw, with which he opened a cabinet. There were many other things too which struck his imagination, and on nearly all the windows he saw his own portrait. "By what strange chance," he said, "do I play a part in these scenes, seeing I was not born when they took place? And what put it into the painter's head to paint a man like me?" Then he saw on the windows a beautiful lady, with a face so full of intelligence that he could not take his eyes off her. There were, besides, endless different figures, and they were all so full of expression that he really thought that what was only represented by a mixture of colours was actually taking place under his own eyes. He did not leave the gallery till it was no longer light enough to distinguish the pictures. When he went back to his room he took up an old manuscript, the first that came to his hand. The leaves were of vellum, with illuminated borders, and the cover of gold, enamelled with blue and covered with ciphers. He was very much astonished to see in the book the same things that were on the windows of the gallery. He tried to read what was written, but found he could not. All at once he saw on one of the pages a picture of musicians singing, in another games of basset and tric-trac, cards being dealt and dice thrown. Turning over the vellum, there he saw an assembly where they were dancing, all the ladies grandly dressed and wonderfully beautiful. Turning over once more, he smelt the odour of a delicious repast, and there he saw little figures eating, the biggest not a quarter-inch high. One of them, turning towards the prince, said: "To your good health, Torticoli. Try to give us back our queen. If you do so, it will be well with you; if not, evil will befall you." At these words the prince was seized with terrible fear; and he trembled so much that at length he let the book fall on one side while he himself fell to the other like a dead man. At the noise of his fall his guards came running. They loved him dearly, and they took every possible means of restoring him to consciousness. When he had recovered enough to speak, they asked him what was the matter. He told them they fed him so insufficiently that he had no strength, and that, having his head full of imaginings, he seemed to see and hear such astonishing things in this book that he had been seized with terror. His guards, in great distress, gave him food in spite of all King Sombre's orders to the contrary. When he had eaten, he took the book, and opening it again in their presence, he found nothing of what he had seen before, which convinced him that he had been mistaken.

Next day he returned to the gallery. Again he saw the paintings on the windows, and the personages in them moved about, walked along paths, hunted stags and hares, fished, built little houses—for all the pictures were very small. And everywhere he saw his own portrait in a dress exactly like his own. The figure was going to the dungeon of the tower to find the golden screw. He thought to himself that as he had eaten well he could no longer suppose that all he saw was a mere vision. "This is too mysterious," he said, "for me to neglect any possible means of knowing more. Perhaps I shall learn something in the dungeon." So he went, and knocking against the wall, one spot seemed to him to give back a hollow sound. Taking a hammer he knocked the plaster down off this part, and found there a golden screw, very finely made. Still ignorant what use to put it to, he saw in a corner of the dungeon an old cupboard of rotten wood. He tried to open it, but he could find no lock. No matter on what side he turned it, it was quite useless. At last he saw a little hole, and having an idea that the screw would be useful here, he put it in. Then pulling energetically he opened the cupboard. But if it was old and ugly outside, it made up for it by its wonderful beauty inside. All the drawers were of cut rock crystal, or amber, or precious stones. When he had drawn out one, he found other smaller ones at the side, above, beneath, and at the back, divided from each other by mother-of-pearl partitions. Pulling out the mother-of-pearl, and then the drawers, he found each one filled with the most beautiful weapons in the world, splendid crowns and wonderful portraits. Prince Torticoli was delighted, and went on pulling out more and more without

stopping. At last he found a little key made of a single emerald with which he opened a little door at the back. He was dazzled by a brilliant carbuncle out of which a large box had been made. He drew out the box hastily, but what was his horror to find it full of blood, and a hand lying in it cut off at the wrist and holding a miniature case. At sight of this Torticoli shuddered, his hair stood on end, and his unsteady legs could hardly support him. Sitting down on the ground with the box still in his hand, but with his eyes turned away from so horrible an object, he had a great desire to put it back in the place from where he had taken it. He thought to himself that in all that had taken place up till now there had been something very mysterious. He remembered what the little figure in the book had said to him, that according to his conduct, evil or good would befall him, and he feared the future no less than the present. Reproaching himself after a time for a cowardice unworthy of a great soul, he made a strong effort, and fixing his eyes on the hand, he said: "O unfortunate hand! Can you not tell me your sad story by some signs? If I am able to serve you, you may rest assured of the generosity of my heart." At these words the hand appeared to be agitated, and moving its fingers, it made signs the sense of which he understood as well as if it had been spoken in articulate words. "You must know," the hand said, "that you can be of the utmost use to him from whom cruel jealousy has separated me. In this portrait you see that beautiful lover for whom I sorrow. Go now at once into the gallery. Watch where the sun's rays strike most keenly. Look there and you will find my treasure." Then the hand stopped moving, and to the various questions the prince asked, it answered nothing. "Where shall I put you?" he asked. It made some signs which the prince understood to mean that it must be put back in the cupboard. This was done, everything was locked up again, the screw hidden in the same wall he had taken it from, and somewhat more at ease among all these wonders, he went down to the gallery. When he entered, the windows began to rattle and shake in an extraordinary fashion.

Looking where the sunbeams were striking, he saw it was on the portrait of a young man, so handsome and with so distinguished an air that it was pleasant to look on him. Raising this picture, he found an ebony panel with gilt mouldings as in the rest of the gallery. He did not know how to take out the panel or even whether he should take it out at all. Looking at the windows, he found that the wainscot could slide up, and raising it at once, he found himself in a vestibule made of porphyry, and decorated with statues. He mounted a wide staircase made of agate, the balustrade of which was of worked gold, and entered a salon made of lapis lazuli. Then walking through endless apartments, where the excellence of the pictures and the richness of the furniture delighted him, he reached at last a little room where all the ornaments were of turquoise. There on a bed of blue gauze and gold he saw a lady who seemed to be asleep. Her beauty was marvellous. Her hair blacker than ebony showed off the whiteness of her skin. She seemed to be restless in her sleep; her face had a wearied look as if she were ill. The prince fearing to wake her, stepped forward softly. She was speaking, and listening eagerly to what she said, he heard these few words, broken by sighs: "Do you think, traitor, that I can love you, after you have taken my dear Trasimene away from me? What! before my very eyes you dared to separate that dear hand from that mighty arm? Is it thus you think to prove to me your respect and your love? Ah, Trasimene, dear lover, shall I never see you any more?" The prince noticed that her tears sought a passage between her closed eyelids, moistening her cheeks like the morning dew.

He stayed at the foot of her bed without moving, not knowing whether he ought to wake her or leave her longer in a sleep in which she seemed so unhappy. He had gathered that Trasimene was her lover, and that it was his hand he had found in the dungeon. A thousand conflicting thoughts were rushing through his mind, when he heard the sound of sweet music, the mingled song of nightingales and canaries, blending so exquisitely as to surpass the most charming human voices. At that moment an eagle of an extraordinary size came in, flying slowly through the air, and holding in its claws a golden branch laden with rubies in the shape of cherries. It looked fixedly at the sleeping beauty, and seemed to see in her its sun, and spreading out its great wings hovered before her, now rising, now falling again to her feet. After some minutes it turned towards the prince, and coming forward placed in his hand the golden branch with the cherries. Then the singing birds sent out such melody as pierced the vaults of the palace. The prince was so watchful of everything that took place that he felt sure the lady was enchanted, and that the honour of

some glorious adventure was reserved for him. Going up to her he knelt down, and touching her with the branch he said: "Fair and charming lady, who sleeps by some power unknown to me, I conjure you to wake up again to life and action." The lady, opening her eyes and seeing the eagle, cried: "Stay, dear lover, stay," but the royal bird uttered a sharp and painful cry, and flew away with his little feathered songsters. The lady then turning to Torticoli, said: "It is my heart rather than my gratitude that now speaks; I know that I owe you everything, and that you are bringing me back to the light I have not seen for two hundred years. The enchanter who loved me, and who brought so many misfortunes on me, has reserved this great adventure for you. It is in my power to serve you, and I have the greatest desire to do so. Tell me what are your desires and I shall employ the fairy art, which is mine in the highest degree, to make you happy." "Madam," answered the prince, "if your knowledge enables you to divine the feelings of the heart, you must know that in spite of the misfortunes that have been heaped on me, I am less to be pitied than another might be." "That is because you have resources in your mind," said the fairy, "but in any case do not force on me the shame of ingratitude. What do you wish for? I can do everything, so ask." "I desire," said Torticoli, "that the handsome Trasimene, for whom you sigh, shall be restored to you." "You are too generous," she answered, "to prefer my interests to your own. This great affair will be achieved by someone else — a lady. I will say no more at present. Only be certain that she will not be indifferent to you. But do not any longer refuse me the pleasure of being of use to you. What are your wishes?" "Madam," said the prince, throwing himself at her feet, "you see my hideous face. I am called Torticoli, in mockery. Make me less ridiculous." "Go, my prince," said the fairy, touching him three times with the golden branch, "go; you will be so accomplished, so perfect, that never man in times past or time to come will be your equal. Call yourself henceforth Peerless, for that name will be yours with just right." The prince, in gratitude, embraced her knees, and by a silence which expressed his joy, left her to guess what was passing in his mind. She made him get up, and when he looked at himself in the mirrors that adorned the room, Peerless no longer recognised Torticoli. He was three feet taller. His hair fell in thick curls on his shoulders. He looked all dignity and grace. His features were regular; his eyes full of intelligence. In short, his person was a piece of workmanship worthy of a kind and tender-hearted fairy. "Why may I not reveal to you your destiny, tell you of the obstacles that fortune will place in your way, and teach you how to avoid them? How delighted I should be to add this service to what I have just done you, but I should be displeasing the higher genius who is guiding you. Go, prince, flee from the tower, and remember that the Fairy Goodheart will always be your friend." At these words she herself, the palace, and the wonders the prince had seen, disappeared, and he found himself in a thick forest, more than a hundred leagues from the tower, where King Sombre had imprisoned him.

Let us leave him to recover from his natural astonishment while we look on at two other scenes. Let us find out what is going on amongst the guards whom his father had sent to watch him, and what is happening to Princess Trognon. The poor guards, astonished that the prince did not ask for supper, entered his room, and not finding him, they searched for him everywhere, terribly afraid lest he should have escaped. Their trouble being all in vain, they were in despair, for they feared that King Sombre who was so cruel would put them to death. After having discussed all the possible ways of appeasing his anger, they came to the conclusion that one of them should go to bed and hide his face, while they would say that the prince was very ill. Shortly afterwards they would pretend he was dead, and they would bury a log and this would get them out of the difficulty. The plan seemed to them perfect, and at once they set about carrying it out. The shortest of the guards had a great hump fastened on to him and went to bed. Then they told the king that his son was very ill, but he thought they only said so to work on his feelings, and he refused to relax any of his severity. This was just what the terrified guards wanted, and the more they pretended to urge him the more indifference did King Sombre show.

As for Princess Trognon, she arrived in a little vehicle no higher than your arm, and which was carried in a litter. King Sombre went to meet her. When he saw how ugly she was, her eyebrows that met each other, her large, flat nose, her mouth stretching round to her ears, he could not help saying: "In truth, Princess Trognon, it is very fitting that you should despise my Torticoli! I confess he is very ugly, but, to tell the truth, he is not so ugly as you." "Your majesty," she answered, "I am not vain enough to take offence at any disagreeable things you may say to me. Perhaps you do so as a sure means of persuading me to love your charming Torticoli: but I declare to you that in spite of my miserable face and my many faults, I do not wish to marry him, and I prefer to be Princess Trognon rather than Queen Torticoli." King Sombre was very angry at this answer. "I assure you," he said, "that I will have no contradiction. The king, your father, should be your master, and he has placed you in my hands." "There are things," she answered, "in which we have the power of choice. It has been against my will that I have been brought here, I give you warning, and I shall look upon you as my worst enemy if you force me to consent." The king, still more angry, left her. She was given an apartment in the palace, where she was waited on by ladies who received orders to convince her that her best part was to marry the prince.

Meanwhile the guards, who feared lest they should be discovered and that the king should come to know that his son had escaped, hastened to tell him he was dead. Hearing this, he was overcome by a grief of which they had not thought him capable. He cried, he shrieked, and venging himself on Trognon for his loss, he sent her to the tower in the place of his dear, lost son. The poor

princess's grief was as great as her astonishment when she found herself a prisoner. She was full of spirit, and she spoke her mind respecting so cruel a proceeding, hoping they would repeat her words to the king; but no one dared to speak to him on the subject. She thought, too, she could write to her father about the bad treatment she received, and then he would come and deliver her; but her attempts in this direction were useless, for they intercepted her letters and gave them to King Sombre. So long as she lived in hopes that her letters would bring her help, she was in less distress, and every day she walked in the gallery to look at the pictures on the windows. Nothing surprised her more than the number of different things which were there represented, and to see pictures of herself. "Since I have been in this country," she said, "the painters have taken a strange pleasure in painting me. Are there not enough ridiculous faces without mine? Or do they wish by placing mine near that young charming shepherdess to enhance her beauty still more by contrasting her with me?" Then she looked at the portrait of a shepherd who was beautiful beyond description. "How much is anyone to be pitied," she said, "whom nature has treated as badly as she has done me! And how happy it must make one to be beautiful!" As she said this the tears stood in her eyes, and catching a glimpse of herself in a mirror, she turned away abruptly. Suddenly to her astonishment she saw behind her a little old woman with a hood on her head, who was even uglier than herself. "Princess," said the old woman, "the choice is given you between virtue and beauty. I have been listening to your touching laments. If you desire beauty, you will be coquettish, vain, and very gay. If you choose to remain as you are, you will be good, respected, and very humble-minded." Trognon looked at the old woman who spoke to her, and asked her if beauty was incompatible with goodness. "No," said the good woman to her, "but so far as you are concerned, it is decreed that you can only have one of them." "Well," said Trognon, in a firm voice, "I prefer my ugliness to beauty." "What! you prefer to frighten those who look at you?" asked the old woman. "Yes, madam," said the princess. "I would rather have every misfortune in the world than fail in virtue." "I have brought my yellow and white muff on purpose," said the fairy. "If you blow on the yellow side, you will be like that beautiful shepherdess whom you thought so charming, and be loved by a shepherd whose portrait you have looked at more than once. If you blow on the white side, you will be strengthened in the path of virtue on which you now set out so courageously." "Ah! madam," answered the princess, "do not refuse me this favour. It will console me for all the contempt I have had poured on me." So the little old woman gave her the muff of virtue and beauty. And Trognon made no mistake, but blowing on the white side, thanked the fairy, who vanished immediately.

Trognon was delighted at the good choice she had made; and however much she might envy the incomparable beauty of the shepherdess on the painted windows, she consoled herself by thinking that beauty passes like a dream, that virtue is an everlasting and unchangeable treasure which endures longer than life. She still had hopes that the king, her father, would head a great army, and come and take her away from the tower. She awaited the moment of his coming with the utmost impatience, and was dying to mount to the turret to see him arrive with the help she looked for. But how could she climb so high? She crawled about in her room more slowly than a tortoise, and when at any time she wanted to mount anywhere, her women had to carry her. However, she hit on a very original plan. Knowing the clock was in the turret, she took the weights off and put herself in their place. When they wound up the clock, she was hoisted to the top. Once there, she looked hastily through the window over the country, but seeing nothing coming, she drew back to rest a little. While she was leaning up against the wall that Torticoli, or, as we should say, Prince Peerless, had broken down and built up again rather badly, the plaster fell and so did the golden screw, rattling on the floor

near Trognon. Seeing it, she picked it up and examined it to find out if it were any use to her. Now, as she was very clever, she saw quickly enough that it was meant to open the cupboard which had no lock. She succeeded in doing this, and was no less delighted than the prince had been on finding all the rare and beautiful things it contained. There were four thousand drawers, all filled with jewels, antique and modern. At last she found the little golden door, the carbuncle box, and the hand swimming in blood. Shuddering, she would have cast it away from her, but it was not in her power to let it go, for a secret attraction prevented her. "Alas!"

she said in distress, "I would rather die than remain longer with this hand." But in a moment she heard a sweet, pleasant voice that said to her: "Take courage, princess; your happiness depends on this adventure." "Ah, what can I do?" she asked, trembling. "You must take this hand into your own room," said the voice, "hide it under your pillow, and when you see an eagle, give it to him without a moment's delay." However frightened the princess was, the voice had something so persuasive about it that she did not hesitate to obey; and so she put back the treasures and curiosities as she had found them without taking a single one. Her guards, who feared that she too had escaped, searched for her, and were very much astonished to find her in a place where she could not, they said, have reached except by enchantment. She was three days without seeing anything of importance. She dared not open the beautiful carbuncle box, for the bleeding hand terrified her too much. At last one night hearing a noise against the window, she drew aside her curtain, and saw by the light of the moon an eagle flying about. She rose as quickly as she could, and dragging herself along the floor, she opened the window. The eagle entered, flapping its wings noisily, as if to express delight. Without a moment's hesitation she gave him the hand, which he seized with his claws, and was gone. In his place was a young man, the handsomest and the comeliest that ever was seen. His brow was wreathed with a diadem, his dress was covered with jewels, and in his hand he held a portrait. It was he who spoke first. "Princess," he said to Trognon, "for two hundred years a wicked enchanter has imprisoned me here. We both of us loved the wonderful Fairy Goodheart (for that is the name of my queen). She favoured me, and he was jealous. His art was greater than mine, and he determined to use it for my ruin. So he told me in a masterful manner that he forbade me to see her any more. Such a command was not in accord either with my love or with my rank, so I defied him; and the fair lady I adore was so offended with the enchanter's conduct, that in her turn she forbade him ever to come near her

again. Then the cruel wretch determined to punish us both. One day when I was with her, in great delight because of a portrait she had given me, and that I was looking at, but thinking it not a thousandth part so beautiful as the original, he appeared, and with a blow from his sabre cut my hand from my arm. Fairy Goodheart felt the pain more keenly than myself, and fell fainting on her bed. All at once I saw I was covered with feathers, and I was changed into an eagle. Every day I was allowed to see the queen, but I could not come near her, nor wake her. I only had the consolation of hearing her uttering constant sighs, and speaking of her dear Trasimene. I also knew that at the end of two hundred years a prince would call back Goodheart to the light of day, and that a princess by restoring me my hand would give me back my former shape. A fairy, who is interested in your fame, has arranged it in this way. It was she who so carefully locked up my hand in the cupboard in the dungeon, she who has given me the power to-day of expressing to you my gratitude. Say, princess, what would give you most pleasure, and it shall be yours at the moment." "Great king," answered Trognon, after some moments of silence, "if I do not reply at once, it is not because I am in doubt as to my desires, but I confess to you that I am little used to such astonishing adventures, and I think it must be a dream rather than a reality." "No, madam," answered Trasimene, "it is no dream. You will see the results of it as soon as you tell me the gifts you wish for." "If I asked all those I stand in need of to make me perfect," she said, "however powerful you may be, it would be difficult to satisfy me. But I really care only for the most essential. Therefore make my soul as beautiful as my body is ugly and deformed." "Ah, princess," cried King Trasimene, "you delight me by a choice so good and worthy. Therefore your body will become as beautiful as your soul and mind." He touched the princess with the portrait of the fairy. She heard her bones go crack, crack. They stretched out, they fitted into their right places. She stood up, tall, beautiful, straight, her skin whiter than milk, her features regular, her bearing at once dignified and modest, her face refined and pleasant. "What wonder is this!" she cried. "Is this I? Is it possible?" "Yes, madam," replied Trasimene, "it is you. The wise choice you made of goodness has brought about the happy change you now experience. What a pleasure for me, after what I owe you, to be destined to help towards it! But now cast away for ever the name of Trognon, and take that of Radiant instead, for you are worthy of it, from your brilliancy and your charms." At that moment he disappeared, and the princess, without knowing by what means she had come, found herself at the edge of a little river, in a shady place, the pleasantest that could anywhere be found.

She had not yet seen herself, but now the water of this stream was so clear, that looking in it, she saw with the greatest surprise, that she was the same shepherdess whom she had admired so much in the windows of the gallery. In truth, like her, she had a white dress trimmed with fine lace, the prettiest ever a shepherdess wore; her girdle was of little roses and jasmine, her hair adorned with flowers. Close to her hand she found a crook, painted and gilded, while a flock of sheep were feeding along the bank. The sheep dog hearing her voice seemed to know her and came up and fawned on her. What could she think of all these fresh wonders! She had been born, and till now she had lived, the ugliest creature imaginable, but then she was a princess. Now she was fairer than the morning star, but she was only a shepherdess; and the loss of her rank she could not but feel somewhat. Worn out by these different thoughts at last she fell asleep. She had been awake all night, as I have already said, and the journey she had taken, although she had not known it, was a hundred leagues long. So she was rather tired. Her sheep and her dog gathered at her side, seemed to be keeping watch over her, and giving her the care she owed to them. The sun could not scorch her though it shone ever so brightly, for the leafy trees protected her, and the delicate, fresh grass on which she had lain down, seemed as if it were proud of so fair a load.

Here the violets thickest bloom
Peeping from their hiding places,
See them lift their little faces,
Breathing out their sweet perfume.

The birds sang together in sweet harmony, and the zephyrs held their breath for fear they should wake her. A shepherd tired out by the heat of the sun, having espied the spot from far off, made for it as quickly as possible, but seeing young Radiant he was so astonished that had it not been for a tree to lean against, he would have fallen on the ground. In truth he recognised her as the same maiden whose beauty he had admired in the gallery windows and in the vellum book: for the reader of course has guessed that the shepherd was Prince Peerless. Some unknown attraction had kept him in this country, and he had been admired by all who had seen him, and among the shepherds he was no less distinguished by his skill in everything, his handsome face, his quick wit, than he had formerly been by his birth. He gazed on Radiant with an eagerness and delight he had never felt till now. He knelt before her, examined all the different points that made of her such a perfect whole, and his heart was the first to pay that tribute which no one since has been able to refuse. While he stayed dreaming near her, Radiant woke up, and seeing Peerless by her side in gay shepherd's dress, she looked at him, and recalled him, for she had seen his portrait in the tower. "Fair shepherdess," he said, "what happy fate has led you here? You come, doubtless, to receive our incense and our vows. Ah, already I feel that I shall be the first to pay my homage." "No, shepherd," she said, "I have no wish to claim honours that are not due to me. I wish to remain a simple shepherdess, for I love my flock and my dog. Solitude has charms for me. I seek for nothing else." "What! young shepherdess, in coming to this spot, you mean to hide yourself from those who dwell here? Is it possible," he went on, "that you are so evilly disposed towards us? At least, accept me, since I am first to offer

my services." "No," replied Radiant, "I do not wish to see you oftener than the others, though already I have an unaccountable feeling of respect for you. But tell me of some good shepherdess with whom I can find a home, for being unknown here, and of an age when I cannot dwell alone, I shall be very glad to have her protection." Peerless was delighted with this commission, and took her to a neat little cabin, charming in its simplicity. There dwelt a little old woman, who very rarely went out, because she could hardly walk. "See, good mother," said Peerless, leading Radiant forward, "here I bring you an incomparable damsel, whose very presence will make you young again." The old woman embraced her, and said in a pleasant voice that she was welcome, that she was sorry to lodge her so poorly, but that at least she would lodge her very well in her heart. "I did not think," said Radiant, "I should find here so kind a welcome and such courtesy. I assure you, good mother, I am delighted to be with you. Do not refuse," she added, turning to the shepherd, "to tell me your name, so that I may know to whom I am obliged for this service." "My name is Peerless," answered the prince, "but at present I do not wish to be called anything but your slave." "And as for me," said the little, old woman, "I wish to know the name of the shepherdess whose host I am." The princess said she was called Radiant, and the old woman seemed charmed with so lovely a name, while Peerless said a hundred pretty things on the subject.

The old shepherdess, fearing lest Radiant should be hungry, brought her a shining earthen vessel, some sweet milk, some brown bread, fresh eggs, newly-churned butter, and cream cheese. Peerless ran to his hut, and brought strawberries, nuts, cherries, and other fruits, all garnished with flowers; and to have the chance of staying longer with Radiant he asked her permission to eat with her. Alas! it would have been difficult to refuse him. She had great pleasure in his company, and however cold she pretended to be she knew quite well that her presence was not a matter of indifference to Peerless.

When he had left her she sat thinking of him for a long time, while his mind was full of her. He saw her every day when he led his flocks into the same pasture where hers were feeding, and where he sang love songs to her. He played the flute and the pipes for her to dance to, which she did with such grace and accuracy as filled him with admiration. Now each of them was thinking a great deal of the series of astonishing adventures which had happened to them, and they both began to be uneasy. Peerless never left her alone if he could help it.

Wherever Radiant went he followed fast,
And while beseeching looks on her he cast,
All the delights and charms of love he told.
Such burning passion could not leave her cold.
But fearing danger, though she knew not why,
She fled whene'er the shepherd she did spy.
'Tis hard to flee when pleasure is in staying—
Peerless had watched at times her eyes betraying
Far other thoughts than hate. But now in vain
He seeks to win some tender look again.

She avoided him with the utmost care, and reproached herself endlessly for her affection for him. "What!" she said, "I am so unhappy as to be in love, and that with a miserable shepherd! What a sad fate is mine! I preferred goodness to beauty, yet it seems heaven in rewarding me for this choice has made me beautiful, but only for my misfortune. Without these vain attractions, this shepherd that I hide from would never have set himself to please me, and I should not have the shame of blushing for my feelings towards him." Her tears left her always filled with sad thoughts, and she was the more troubled at seeing the misery of her dear shepherd.

He too was overcome with melancholy. He wished to declare to Radiant the greatness of his birth, in the hopes that she would be perhaps influenced by vanity, and would listen to him more willingly. But after all he thought she might not believe him, and if she asked for some proof, he had no means of giving her such. "How cruel is my lot!" he cried. "Although before I was hideous to look at, at all events I was my father's heir, and a great kingdom makes up for many faults. Now it would be useless to present myself either to him or to his subjects, for none of them would recognise me, and all the kind Fairy Goodheart has done for me in taking away my name and my ugliness, ends in making me a shepherd, and placing me under the spell of an unkind shepherdess who cannot endure me. O cruel star," he said with a sigh, "shine on me with more favour, or give me back my deformity and with it my former carelessness!"

Such were the sad laments of the lover and his mistress, each ignorant of the truth about the other. But one day when Radiant had been doing her best to keep out of Peerless's way, he on the contrary had made up his mind to speak to her, and to have a pretext which should not offend her. So he took a little lamb, decked it with ribbons and flowers, and put on it a collar of coloured straw worked so beautifully that it was a master-piece. He himself had a mantle of rose-coloured taffeta, trimmed with English lace. Thus with his crook decked with ribbons and his scrip slung over his shoulder, all the Aladdins in the world would have made but a poor show beside him.

He found Radiant sitting on the bank of a stream, which flowed slowly through the thickest part of the wood. Her sheep were scattered here and there, for the melancholy of the shepherdess prevented her caring for them. Peerless greeted her timidly, giving her the little lamb, and looking at her tenderly. "What have I done, fair shepherdess," he said, "to be so marked out for your hatred? You blame your eyes if they so much as look at me, and you seek to flee me. Is my love for you such a crime? Can you ever hope to be loved with more purity or faithfulness? Have not my words and my actions shown my respect and the warmth of my feeling? But doubtless you love some one else. Your heart already belongs to another." But she answered him:

"Shepherd, list, an you would know
Why henceforth I flee you,
My poor heart is troubled so,
When my eyes do see you.

"If, perchance, I loved you less
Hardly would I hide me,
But since all my looks confess,
I fear what may betide me.

"Duty I would bid begone
While you near me hover;
Slowly drag the footsteps on
When one flees a lover.

"Fare you well, and, for my peace,
Fare you well for ever!
Leaving you, my life may cease,
Yet—here our ways must sever."

And so saying, Radiant moved away. The prince, full of love and despair, would have followed her, but his grief became so great that he fell unconscious at the foot of a tree. Ah, severe and too-timid virtue, why do you fear a man who has loved you from his tenderest years? He is incapable of doing you wrong, and his affection is altogether innocent. But the princess distrusted herself as much as him. She could not but own the merits of this charming shepherd, and she knew well how necessary it is to avoid what we are tempted to love too much.

No harder task could have been hers at that moment, tearing herself away from the person she loved more tenderly and more dearly than any one she had ever seen. She could not help turning her head sometimes just to look if he were following, and she saw him fall down as if dead. She loved him, yet she would not give herself the consolation of going to his aid. When she was on the plain she lifted her eyes piteously, and clasping her hands, cried: "O virtue! O glory! O high estate! See how I sacrifice my happiness to you! O fate! O Trasimene! I give up my fatal beauty. Give me back my former ugliness, or give me back, without the need to blush for it, the lover whom I leave behind." Then she stopped, hesitating whether to flee or to return. Her heart called to her to go back to the wood where she had left Peerless; but her virtue was stronger than her tenderness, and she took the generous determination not to see him.

Since she had been living in these parts, she had heard tell of an enchanter who dwelt with his sister in a castle he had built on the borders of the island. Their fairy lore was the talk of every one, and every day new wonders came to light. She felt that it must be a magic power at least that should blot out of her heart the picture of the charming shepherd, and without saying a word to her kind hostess who had received her and treated her as a daughter, she set off, her mind so full of her troubles that she never thought of the danger there might be in so young and beautiful a maiden travelling all by herself. She stopped neither night nor day, neither ate nor drank, in such haste was she to reach the castle and be cured of her love. But passing through a wood she heard some one singing, and it seemed as if she heard her name uttered in the voice of one of her companions. Stopping to listen she heard these words:

"The comeliest shepherd of the plain was Peerless,
And all his heart on Radiant fast was set,
Proud of his love, and confident, and fearless,
He poured his passion out whene'er they met.
But his young mistress of his love made light,
Though when her lover wandered from her sight,
She'd sigh and sigh until he came again;
And ne'er such sigh for him was heaved in vain.
Upon the grass together they would sit,
And what was taught him by his love and wit
He'd sing and pipe the summer morning long,
And stop to hear from her sweet mouth his song."

"Ah! but this is too bad," she said, shedding tears. "Ah, treacherous shepherd, you have boasted of the harmless favour I have granted you! You dared to think my weak heart would be more ready to listen to your love than my own duty. You have spoken your wicked desires aloud, and yours is the fault that my name is sung in the woods and the plains." And at that moment

she felt so very angry that she thought she could have looked upon him with indifference, and perhaps even with hatred. "It is useless," she said, "for me to go farther to seek a remedy for my ill. I have nothing to fear from a shepherd whom I know to be so undeserving. I shall return to the hamlet with that shepherdess I have been listening to." She called her as loud as she could, but there came no answer, yet nevertheless from time to time she heard some one singing near her. She became uneasy and afraid. The truth was, this wood belonged to the enchanter, and no one could

pass through it without meeting with some sort of adventure. Radiant, more uncertain than ever, hastened on her way out of the wood. "Has the shepherd whom I feared become of so little consequence to me now that I should permit myself to see him again? Is it not rather that my heart, in league with him, is seeking to deceive me? Oh! let me flee, let me flee away; it is the best thing an unhappy princess like me can do." So she went on her way to the enchanter's castle; and once there she entered without hindrance. She crossed several great courts, where the grass and the bramble-bushes grew so high, that you would have thought no one had walked there for a hundred years, and when she pushed them aside her hands were full of scratches. She went into a hall, where the daylight only came through a little hole, and which was hung with bats' wings. Twelve cats, suspended from the ceiling, served as a chandelier, and made mewling enough to drive any one distracted. On a long table there were twelve big mice fastened down by their tails, with a piece of lard lying before each of them, which they could not reach. The mice were in terror of the cats, and were dying of hunger within sight of good pieces of lard. The princess was thinking of the suffering of these animals when she saw the enchanter come in in a long black robe. On his head for a cap he wore a crocodile, and never was so terrible a headdress seen. The old man wore spectacles, and held a whip in his hand made of twenty long serpents, all alive. Oh, how frightened the princess was! How she longed at that moment for her shepherd, her sheep, and her dog! Her only thought was of flight, and without a word to this terrible man, she ran to the door. But the door was all covered with spiders' webs. She took one away, and found another. She took that away, and found a third. When she took the third away a new one appeared in front of still another. In fact, these tiresome spider-web curtains were altogether numberless. The poor princess came to an end of her strength, and her arms were not strong enough to support the webs. She wished to sit down on the ground to rest for a little, but there she felt long thorns

going into her. Jumping up again, she tried once more to get out, but ever another web appeared when she had torn the first away. The wicked old man looked on at her all the while, laughing as if he would choke. At last he called to her, saying: "You may spend the rest of your life trying, but you will never succeed. You seem to be young, and you are the prettiest of all pretty things. If you like, I will marry you. I will give you these twelve cats you see hanging from the ceiling to do what you like with, and those twelve mice on the table will be yours too. The cats are princes, and the mice princesses. The minxes, at different times, have had the honour to be loved by me, for I have always been amiable and gallant, but none of them would marry me. The princes were my rivals, and happier than I. I was seized with jealousy. I found the means of enticing them here, both princes and princesses, and as they were caught they were turned into cats or mice. The fun of it is that they hate each other just as much as they used to love each other, and what more perfect vengeance could I find?" "Ah, sire," said Radiant, "turn me into a mouse. I deserve it just as much as these poor princesses." "What!" said the magician, "you will not love me, then, you little Bo-peep?" "I have made up my mind to love no one," she answered. "Oh, you little silly!" said he. "I shall give you such nice things to eat. I shall tell you stories, and give you the prettiest clothes in the world. You will always drive in a coach, or be carried in a litter, and you will be called madam." "I have made up my mind to love no one," replied the princess once more. "Take care what you are saying," cried the enchanter angrily. "You will long repent of this." "No matter," said Radiant, "I have made up my mind to love no one." "Oh, very well, coldhearted creature," said he, touching her; "since you will not love anybody, you shall be turned into a special kind of animal. Henceforth you shall be neither flesh nor fish. You shall have neither blood nor bones. Because you are still in your fresh youth, you shall be green; you shall be light and nimble; you shall live in the meadows as you lived before, and your name shall be Grasshopper." At that instant

Princess Radiant was turned into the prettiest grasshopper in the world and, regaining her liberty, she made off at once for the garden.

As soon as she was free to utter her laments, she cried in distress: "This then is what your promises end in, Trasimene! Was it this sad fate you kept for me two hundred years long? A beauty as little lasting as the flowers of spring, and in the end a covering of green crape, a queer little body, neither flesh nor fish, and with neither blood nor bones! I am indeed unhappy! Alas! a crown would have hidden all my defects. I would have found a husband worthy of me, and if I had remained as shepherdess, dear Peerless's one desire would have been to win my heart. He is but too well revenged for my cruel contempt. Here I am, a grasshopper, fated to sing day and night, when my heart full of bitterness would rather bid me weep." So spoke the grasshopper hidden amongst the delicate grass on the edge of the stream.

But what was Prince Peerless doing away from his beloved shepherdess? The cruel manner in which she had left him pained him so much that he had not the strength to follow her. Before he could have reached her, he had fainted, and he remained for a long time quite unconscious at the foot of the tree where Radiant had seen him fall, till at length the coolness of the ground, or some unknown power, brought him back to life. He did not dare to go to her cottage that day. Turning over in his mind some of the last verses she had said to him—

"If perchance I loved you less
Hardly would I hide me"—

he began to be more hopeful, and felt sure that with time and care he would breed in her a little gratitude. But what were his thoughts when, going to the old shepherdess's hut where Radiant lodged, he learnt that she had not been there since the day before? He was like to die for anxiety, and took his leave full of troubled thoughts. As

he sat grieving by the river-side, he felt over and over again the impulse to throw himself in, and to end his troubles with his life. At last, taking a small dagger, he carved these verses on the bark of a beamtree:

"Clear stream that wanders through the valleys fair,
Green meadow lands that once my pleasure were,
But now my misery,
She whom I loved, and whom you sure have taken
As model for your charms, has now forsaken
Both you and me.
Henceforth my business in this world is sorrow—
From dawn to dusk, again from eve to morrow,
What but to weep?
Young tree, upon whose tender bark I write.
The story of my love and of her flight
In letters deep,
Forgive the pain. Your wounds are records weak
Of what is branded on my spirit meek
In marks of fire.
Her name is rather your adorning; while I—
Now she is gone, to lay me down and die
Is my desire."

He could write no more, for at that moment he was accosted by a little old woman who wore a ruff round her neck, a farthingale, a fillet about her white hair, and a velvet hood. There was something venerable about her antique air. "My son," she said, "the words you utter are very bitter. I beg of you to tell me what is the cause of your sorrow." "Alas! good mother," said Peerless, "I deplore the absence of a lovely shepherdess who has fled from me. I have resolved to seek for her throughout the whole earth, till so be I have found her." "Go in yonder direction, my child," she said, pointing to the road leading to the castle where poor

Radiant had been turned into a grasshopper. "I have a feeling that you will not have to search for her long." Peerless thanked her, and begged that the God of Love would look kindly on her.

The prince met with no other adventure on his way to stop him, but on reaching the wood near the castle of the magician and his sister, he thought he saw the shepherdess. He hastened to follow her, but she still went on "Radiant," he cried, "Radiant, whom I adore, stay a little, deign to hear me!" The phantom sped on faster, and in this pursuit the day went by. When night came on, he saw lights sparkling in the castle, and he thought to himself the shepherdess was perhaps inside. So he ran, and entered without hindrance. Going upstairs, he found in a magnificent hall an old fairy, tall and horribly thin. Her eyes were like two lamps whose light had been put out, and you could see through her cheeks. Her arms were like lathes, her fingers like spindles; a leathery skin covered her skeleton form. Yet, all the same, she had put rouge and patches on her cheeks, and wore green and pink ribbons, a mantle of silver brocade, a crown of diamonds on her head, and jewels all over.

"At last, my prince," she said, "you reach the spot where I have been waiting for you long. Think no more of your little shepherdess. A love so unfitting your rank should make you blush. I am the Queen of the Meteors. I wish you well, and I can be of endless service to you if you will love me." "Love you, madam!" cried the prince, looking at her indignantly. "Love you, madam! Am I master of my heart? No, I could never consent to such unfaithfulness, and I feel even that were I to change the object of my love, you would not take her place. Choose amongst your meteors some influence that pleases you. Love the air, or the winds, but leave mortals in peace."

The fairy was enraged. Waving her hand twice, she filled the gallery with horrible monsters, against whom the young prince had to defend himself with his skill and courage. Some of them had several heads and several arms; others had the face of

a centaur or a siren; some were lions with men's faces, some were sphinxes, and flying dragons. Peerless had nothing but his crook and a small spear which he had armed himself with at the beginning of his journey. From time to time the tall fairy would make the fray to cease, and ask him if he loved her. And always he said he had vowed to be a faithful lover, and he could not change. Tired out with his persistence, she made Radiant appear. "Well," she said, "you see your mistress at the foot of this gallery. Think what you are doing. If you refuse to marry me she will be torn to pieces by tigers before your eyes." "Ah! madam," cried the prince, throwing himself at her feet, "I would willingly die to save my mistress. Spare her life by taking mine." "It is not a question of your death, traitor," replied the fairy, "it is a question of your heart and your hand." While they were speaking the prince heard the voice of his shepherdess as if she were mourning. "Will you let me be devoured?" she said. "If you love me make up your mind to do what the queen commands you." The poor prince hesitated. "Ah, Goodheart," he cried, "have you then forsaken me, after so many promises? Come, come and help us." Hardly had he uttered the words when he heard a voice saying these words distinctly:

"Let fate take its course; only be faithful,
and seek the Golden Branch."

The tall fairy who had thought she had won the day by means of so many different illusions, was in despair at finding such a powerful obstacle across her path as the protection of Goodheart. "Get out of my sight, you miserable stubborn prince!" she cried. "Since your heart is so enflamed, be a cricket, friend of the heat and of the fire." And at that moment the handsome, the splendid Prince Peerless became a little black cricket, who would have burnt himself alive in the first fireplace or the first oven, if he had not called to mind the friendly voice that had bidden him hope. "I must seek the Golden Branch," he said, "and then perhaps I shall regain my own shape. Ah, if I could but find my shepherdess, what would be lacking for perfect happiness?"

The cricket made haste out of the fatal palace, and without knowing where he should go. He recommended himself to the care of the beautiful Fairy Goodheart. Then he took his departure without baggage and without noise, for a cricket fears neither robbers nor misadventures by the way. At his first resting-place, which was in the hollow of a tree, he found a grasshopper in a melancholy condition and unable to sing. The cricket, having no idea that this was a reasoning intelligent being said: "And whither is Gammer Grasshopper bound for?" "And you, Gaffer Cricket, whither away?" This answer very much astonished the love-sick cricket. "What," he cried, "you can speak?" "What? well, I like that!" she cried. "Do you think a grasshopper should be less privileged than a cricket?" "I can speak perfectly well," said the cricket, "because I am a man." "According to that," answered the grasshopper, "I should be able to speak better than you, because I am a woman." "Is then your lot like mine?" said the cricket. "Yes, it must be the same," answered the grasshopper. "But now tell me where you are going." "I should be delighted," the cricket went on, "if we could bear each other company for a long while. I heard a voice which came from I know not where, which said:

'Let fate take its course, and seek the Golden Branch.'

It seemed to me it could only be meant for me. So without delay I set off, though I know not whither I am bound."

This conversation was interrupted by two mice running as fast as ever they could. Seeing a hole at the foot of the tree, they flew in there head foremost, and all but choked the cricket and the grasshopper, who took refuge as they could in a little corner. "Ah, madam," said the biggest mouse, "I have a pain in my side with having run so fast. How does your highness?" "I wrenched

off my tail," said the other. "Otherwise I should still be fastened to the old wizard's table. Did you see how he ran after us? How lucky we are to have got away from his wretched palace!" "I am just a little afraid of the cats and the rat-trap, princess," said the big mouse, "and I fervently wish I may soon reach the Golden Branch." "You know the way then?" said the mouse princess. "Do I know it? I should think I do, madam, as well as the way to my own house," answered the other. "This branch is wonderful. You want only one of its leaves to be rich for ever. It supplies you with money. It breaks the charms of magic. It gives beauty, and

preserves youth. So before daybreak let us set out on the road." "We shall have the honour of your company, this good cricket here and myself, if you are agreeable, ladies," said the grasshopper, "for we also are like you, pilgrims to the Golden Branch." The two parties exchanged compliments with each other. The mice, be it understood, were princesses whom this wicked enchanter had attached to the table; and as for the cricket and the grasshopper, their courtesy most clearly showed their rank.

All of them woke early next morning, and set off together very silently, for they feared lest any hunters on the watch, hearing them speak, might take them and put them into cages. At last they arrived at the Golden Branch. It was in the middle of a wonderful garden, the walks of which were strewn with little Eastern pearls, rounder than peas, instead of sand. The roses were of pink diamonds, and the leaves of emeralds, the pomegranate flowers of garnets, the marigolds of topazes, the jonquils of yellow brilliants, the blue-bottles of turquoises, the tulips of amethysts, opals, and diamonds. In fact, endless were the number and the variety of these beautiful flowers, and they shone brighter than the sun.

Here it was then, as I have already said, the Golden Branch, the same that Prince Peerless received from the eagle, and with which he touched Fairy Goodheart when she was enchanted. It had grown as high as the tallest trees, and was loaded with rubies, which hung from it like cherries. As soon as the cricket, the grasshopper, and the two mice came near it, they took their own natural shapes again. What joy for them! And what delight did not the prince feel at the sight of his fair shepherdess! He threw himself at her feet, and was in the midst of telling her how happy this pleasant and so little expected surprise made him when Queen Goodheart and King Trasimene appeared in such splendour as was in keeping with the magnificence of the garden. Four Cupids armed from top to toe, bows by their sides, quivers on their shoulders, supported with their arrows a little pavilion of

gold and blue brocade, beneath which two beautiful crowns were seen. "Come, dear lovers," cried the queen, stretching out her arms; "come and receive from our hands the crowns which your virtue, your birth and your faithfulness deserve. Your pains are going to be turned into pleasures. Princess Radiant," she said, "this is the prince who was destined for you by your father and his. He did not die in the tower. Take him for your husband, and leave to me the care of your peace and happiness." The princess in great delight threw herself on Goodheart's neck, and seeing her tearful face the fairy understood that it was excess of joy that took from her the power of speech. Peerless threw himself on his knees before the generous fairy. He kissed her hands respectfully, and poured out his thanks in great confusion. Trasimene smiled kindly at him, and Goodheart told them then how she had scarcely ever left them, that it was she who had proposed to Radiant to blow into the yellow and white muff, that she had taken the form of an old peasant, so that the princess might lodge with her, and that it was again she who had told the prince in which direction he should follow his shepherdess. "In truth," she went on, "you have had troubles which I would have saved you if I had been able to. But, after all, the pleasures of love are worth their price." A soft symphony was heard murmuring around them, and the Loves made haste to crown the young lovers. The marriage took place, and while this ceremony was going on, the two princesses, who had just lost their mouse shape, conjured the fairy to use her power to deliver from the wizard's castle the unfortunate mice and cats who were languishing there. "This is too memorable a day," said she, "to refuse you anything." With that she struck the Golden Branch three times, and all who had been imprisoned in the castle made their appearance in their own natural shape, and found their mistresses again. The generous fairy, wishing that every one should have a share in the rejoicing, gave them the cupboard in the dungeon to share between them. This present was worth more than ten kingdoms in those days.

Their pleasure and their gratitude can easily be imagined. Goodheart and Trasimene finished the great work with a generosity which surpassed all they had ever done before, declaring that the palace and the garden of the Golden Branch would in future belong to King Peerless and Queen Radiant. A hundred kings paid tribute to them, and they had a hundred dependent kingdoms.

The Good Little Mouse

ONCE upon a time there lived a king and a queen who loved each other so very, very much that they were all in all to each other. The one always knew what was in the other's mind and heart. Every day they hunted hares and stags in the forest, or fished for soles and carps in the river, or went to balls or to grand banquets where they ate roast meats and sugar-plums, or to the play or the opera. They laughed and sang and invented all kinds of games to amuse themselves. In short, never were any two people so happy. And their subjects followed their example, and each man was merrier than his fellow. For all these reasons this kingdom was called the Land of Joy.

Now King Joyous had a neighbour who lived in quite a different way. He was the sworn enemy of every kind of pleasure, and only took delight in fighting and quarrelling. There was always a scowl on his face; his beard was long, and his eyes were hollow. He was skinny and shrunken, and always clad in black; and his greasy, dirty hair stood on end. His amusement was to see the passers-by knocked down and killed. Criminals he hung with his own hands, and to torture them gave him the keenest joy. Whenever he heard of a good mother who loved her little girl or boy, he sent for her, and before her eyes he broke their arms or wrung their necks. This kingdom was called the Land of Tears.

The fame of King Joyous's happiness came to the ears of the wicked king, who was very envious, and who made up his mind to levy a great army and go and fight his neighbour, and press him hard, till he should be dead or seriously wounded. From all parts he gathered recruits. He collected arms, and ordered cannons to be made. Then everybody was terrified, and said: "Whomsoever this wicked king attacks he will give no quarter to."

When all his preparations were made he marched towards King Joyful's country, who, hearing the evil tidings, immediately set about defending himself. The queen nearly died of fright. "Sire," she said, weeping, "we must flee. Get all the money you can, and we shall go away to the other end of the world." But the king answered: "Madam, I have too much courage for that. I would rather die than be a coward." So, gathering his men round him, he bade the queen a tender farewell; and, mounting his beautiful steed, rode away.

When he was lost to her sight she began to weep sadly, and clasping her hands, she said: "Alas! for the child that is to be born to me! If the king is killed in the wars, I shall be a widow and a prisoner, and the wicked king will harm me in every possible way." So for this thought she could neither eat nor sleep. The king used to write to her every day, but one morning when she was looking over the battlements she saw a courier riding at full speed. "Ho, courier?" she called. "What news?" "The king is dead," he cried, "the battle is lost; and the wicked king will be here in a moment." The poor queen fell down in a swoon. They bore her away and laid her on her bed, while all her women stood round, here one weeping for her father, there another for her son. It was the saddest of all sights.

And now, all at once, they heard shrieks of murder and pillage! It was the wicked king come with all his miserable people, and they were killing without distinction all who came in their way. He entered the palace armed to the teeth, and went to the queen's chamber. When she saw him come in, she was so terrified that she hid herself in her bed, and put the coverlet over her head. Twice or thrice he called her, but she answered not a word. Then he got angry, and in a great rage he said: "I verily

believe you are laughing at me. Do you know that your life is in my hands at this moment?" And, finding where she was, he snatched her cap off her head, so that her lovely hair fell down over her shoulders, and twisting it three times round in his hand, strung her up on his back by it like a sack of wheat. So he carried her off on his great black horse. She begged for mercy, but he only laughed, and said: "Cry then, and make your moan. It only amuses me, and makes me laugh."

He took her away to his own country, vowing all the time he would hang her. But his people told him it would be a pity, for a child would soon be born to her. When he knew that, it occurred to him that if the child were a daughter he might wed her with his son, and, to know which it would be, he sent for a fairy who dwelt on the borders of his kingdom. When she had come, he treated her more hospitably than was his custom; and then took her up into a tower, at the top of which the poor queen had a little scantily-furnished room. Her bed was a mattress not worth a penny, laid on the floor, and there she wept day and night. When the fairy saw her she was deeply touched and, making her a curtsey, whispered while she embraced her: "Take courage, madam; your sorrows will not last for ever. I hope to be of service to you." The queen, somewhat consoled by these words, kissed her, and begged her to take pity on a poor princess, who once had enjoyed a great fortune, and had seen it all vanish away. They were speaking together when the wicked king interrupted them with: "Come along now, don't make such a fuss; I brought you here to tell me whether this slave is to bear a boy or a girl." The fairy answered: "A girl, and she will be the most beautiful and the most accomplished princess that ever was seen." She then wished the child endless gifts and honours. "If she is not beautiful and accomplished," said the wicked king, "I will hang her to her mother's neck, and I will hang her mother on a tree, and no one shall hinder me." And so saying he went out along with the fairy, without casting a glance at the good queen, who was weeping bitterly. "For, alas!" she said to herself, "what can I do? If I have a pretty little girl, he will give her to his monkey of a son, and if she is ugly he will hang both of us. What an unhappy lot is mine! Could I not hide her somewhere, so that he might never see her?"

The time of the little princess's birth was drawing near, and the anxieties of the queen grew worse every day. She had no one to share her grief with, or to console her. The gaoler who guarded her only gave her three peas cooked in water the whole day long, with a little morsel of black bread. She became thinner than a herring, till she was nothing but skin and bone. One evening while she was spinning for the wicked king, who was a great miser and made her work day and night, she saw a very pretty little mouse come in through a hole. "Alas, little one," she said, "what are you seeking here? I have only three peas for my food all the day long, so, if you don't like fasting, run away." The little mouse ran here and there, dancing and cutting capers like a little monkey, and the queen was so amused that she gave it the only pea she had left for her supper. "Here, little one," she said, "eat this; I have no more, but I give it you with a good will." As soon as she had done this, she saw on the table an excellent partridge, exquisitely cooked, and two pots of jam. "In truth," she said, "the good one does is never lost." She ate a little, but her appetite had gone through long fasting. She threw some sweets to the mouse, and it munched them up, and then began to jump about in a livelier way than it had done before supper. Next morning early the gaoler brought the queen's three peas, having put them in a large dish just to mock her. The little mouse came softly and ate them all up, and the bread too. When the queen wished to dine, she found nothing left, and she was very angry with the mouse. "It is a naughty little beast," she said, "and if it goes on doing this I shall die of hunger." When she went to cover up the large dish, which was empty, she found in it all kinds of good things to eat. But while she was eating, the thought came to her that in two or three days perhaps the wicked king would put her child to death, and she rose from the table to weep. Then, lifting her eyes to heaven, she said: "Are there no means of escape?" As she said this she saw the little mouse playing with long pieces of straw. Picking them up, she began to work. "If I have straw enough," she said, "I shall make a covered basket to put my little girl in, and I will give her through the window to the first charitable person who will take care of her." She set to work, therefore, with a good heart. She had plenty of straw, for the mouse was always dragging some into the room, and jumping about all the while. At meal-times the queen gave it her three peas, and found in exchange all sorts of dishes. This astonished her very much, and she never stopped wondering who could be sending her such excellent things.

The queen was looking through the window one day, to see how long the cord should be which she must fasten to the basket to let it down, when, below, she saw a little old woman leaning on a staff, who said to her: "I know your trouble, madam, and if you like I will help you." "Alas! dear friend," said the queen, "you will do me a great service if you come every evening to the foot of the tower. I shall let down my poor child to you. You will feed it, and I shall try to pay you well, if I am ever rich." "I am not fond of money," the old woman answered, "but I like good things to eat. There is nothing I care so much for as a fine plump mouse. If you find any in your garret, kill them, and throw them down to me. I shall not be ungrateful, and your baby will thrive well." When the queen heard this she began to cry, and did not say a word in reply, and the old woman, after waiting for some time, asked her why she was weeping. "Because," she said, "only one mouse comes to my room, and it is so pretty and so sweet that I cannot make up my mind to kill it." "What!" said the old woman, angrily, "you care more for a silly little mouse that gnaws at everything than the child that is to be born to you! Very well, madam, you are not to be pitied. Remain, if you wish, in such good company. I shall find plenty of mice without you; I haven't the least doubt about that." And she went away scolding and muttering.

Although the queen found a nice meal prepared for her, and the mouse came and danced before her, she never once lifted her eyes from the ground where she had fixed them, and the tears ran down her cheeks. That night a princess was born, a miracle of beauty; and, instead of crying as other children do, she smiled to her dear mother, holding out her little hands as if she understood everything. The queen caressed and kissed her with great tenderness, thinking sadly: "Poor darling! Dear child, if you fall into the hands of the wicked king it is all over with you." So she put her in the basket, with a label fastened to her swaddling clothes, on which was written:

This unhappy little girl is called Joliette;

and when she had left her for a moment without looking at her she opened the basket again, and found her much prettier still. Then she kissed her and wept yet more bitterly, not knowing what she should do.

But now the little mouse comes, and gets into the basket with Joliette. "Ah, little creature," said the queen, "it has cost me much to save your life. Perhaps I may lose my dear Joliette. Anyone else would have killed you and given you over to the old glutton, but I could not consent." "Do not repent of what you have done, madam," began the mouse; "I am not so unworthy of your friendship as you may think." The queen was half dead with fright at hearing the mouse talk, but her terror grew much worse when she saw its little snout taking the form of a face, its paws becoming hands and feet, and its whole body growing suddenly larger. At last the queen, who hardly dared to look any more, recognised in the mouse the fairy who had come with the wicked king, and who had treated her so tenderly.

"I wished to test your heart," said the fairy; "I know now it is good, and that you are capable of friendship. We fairies, though we possess immense treasures and riches, seek love as the only consolation in life, and we find it rarely." "Is it possible, fair lady," said the queen, embracing her, "that, being so rich and powerful as you are, you have difficulty in finding friends?" "Yes," she answered, "for we are only loved because it is to people's advantage to show us affection, and we do not care for that. But when you loved me in the shape of a little mouse you had no selfish motive. Then I wished to put you to a still harder test, and so I took the form of an old woman. It was I who talked to you at the foot of the tower, and you then, as always, were true to me." So saying she embraced the queen, kissed the little princess's forehead three times, and said: "My gifts to you, my daughter, are, that you be your mother's comfort, that you be richer than your father, and that you live for a hundred years, ever beautiful, never ill, never wrinkled, never old." The queen in great delight thanked her, and begged her to take Joliette away and care for her, adding that she gave her the child for a daughter.

The fairy accepted the gift and thanked the queen. Putting the little one into the basket she let it down. But she stopped for an instant to change herself into a little mouse again, and when she went down herself afterwards by the cord the child was not to be found. She mounted again in a great fright. "All is lost," she said to the queen; "my enemy, Cancaline, has carried off the princess. You must know that there is a cruel fairy who hates me, and unhappily, being older than I, she has more power. I do not know how to get Joliette out of her wicked clutches."

When the queen heard such sad news she thought she must die of grief. She wept very bitterly, and begged her good friend to do what she could to find the little one again, at whatever cost.

But meanwhile the gaoler came to the queen's room, and, finding that the child had been born, he went to tell the king, who hastened to demand the princess. But she told him that a fairy, whose name she did not know, had come and taken her away by force. Now the wicked king stamped his foot and bit his nails till he had none left. "I told you I should hang you," he said, "and I am going to keep my promise at once." At the word he dragged the poor queen into a wood, climbed up a tree, and was just going to hang her when the fairy made her invisible, and, giving him a great shove, made him fall from the top of the tree, breaking four of his teeth. While they were trying to mend them, the fairy bore the queen away in a flying car to a beautiful castle, where she took great care of her. If only she had had the Princess Joliette with her she would have been quite happy, but it was impossible to discover where Cancaline had hidden her, though the little mouse did her very best.

Time went on, and softened the queen's great sorrow. Fifteen years had already gone by, when a rumour was spread abroad that the wicked king's son was going to marry his turkey-herd, though the little creature was unwilling. It was very surprising that

a turkey-herd should refuse to be queen; nevertheless the wedding garments were got ready, and to see such a beautiful wedding people came from a hundred leagues round. The little mouse went too, wishing to see the turkey-herd at her leisure. Going into the poultry-house she found her dressed in coarse linen, bare-footed, and with a dirty cloth on her head. There were gold and silver garments, and diamonds, and pearls, and ribbons and laces lying on the ground; the turkeys were trampling on them, making them filthy, and spoiling them. The little herd was sitting on a large stone, while the wicked king's son, who was deformed, blind, and lame, was saying rudely: "If you will not give me your heart, I shall

kill you." But she answered, proudly: "I shall not marry you; you are too ugly. And you are like your cruel father. Leave me alone with my little turkeys—I like them better than all your finery." The little mouse looked at her with admiration, for she was as beautiful as the sun. As soon as the wicked king's son went away, the fairy took the form of an old shepherdess, and said: "Good-day, little one; what fine fat turkeys you have got here!" The young turkey-herd looked at this old woman with eyes full of gentleness, and said: "They want me to leave them for a miserable crown—what do you say about it?" "My little girl," said the fairy, "a crown is a very fine thing; you neither know the value nor the weight of it." "Oh, yes, I do," the herd replied, promptly, "and for that reason I will never wear it. But I do not know who I am, nor who my father is, nor my mother. I have neither parents nor friends." "You have beauty and goodness, my child," said the wise fairy, "and these are better than ten kingdoms. Tell me, I beg you, who brought you here, since you have neither father, mother, relations, nor friends?" "It was a fairy called Cancaline who was the cause of my coming here. She used to beat me, and would knock me down without any cause or reason. So one day I ran away, and, not knowing where to go, I stopped in a wood. The wicked king's son came to walk there, and he asked me if I should like to go and be a servant in his yard. I was quite willing, so I had the turkeys given to my charge. He used to come constantly to see them, and he saw me too. Alas, without any desire on my side, he has fallen so very much in love with me that he will not leave me alone."

The fairy, hearing this, began to think the turkey-herd must be Princess Joliette; so she said to her: "Tell me your name, my daughter." "My name is Joliette, at your service." Then the fairy no longer doubted but that it was she, and, throwing her arms round her neck, she was like to have smothered her with caresses. Thereupon she said to her: "Joliette, I have known you for a long time; I am glad you are so good, and so well-bred; but I would wish you to be cleaner, for you are like a little scullion. Here, take these pretty clothes and put them on."

Joliette, who was very obedient, at once cast away the dirty clothes; and, shaking her head a little, her hair, which was fair as sunlight and fine as golden threads, covered her from head to foot, falling in curls to the ground. Then taking in her delicate hands some water from a stream that ran near the poultry-house, she washed her face, which became as fair as an Eastern pearl. It seemed as if roses were blowing on her cheeks and lips, and her sweet mouth breathed the scent of thyme from the woods and the gardens. Her figure was straighter than a reed. In winter you might have taken her skin for snow, in summer for lilies.

When she was adorned with the diamonds and the beautiful clothes, the fairy thought her a miracle of beauty, and said to her: "Who do you think you are, dear Joliette, for you look a very fine lady now?" "In truth," she answered, "I think I am the daughter of some great king." "Would you be very pleased if this were so?" said the fairy. "Yes, good mother," replied Joliette, with a curtsey. "Very well," said the fairy," be easy in your mind then; I shall tell you more to-morrow."

In haste she repaired to her beautiful castle, where the queen was busy spinning silk. The little mouse called to her: "Your majesty, will you give me your distaff and your spindle for the best news you could ever hear?" "Alas!" said the queen, "since the death of King Joyous, and the loss of my Joliette, I wouldn't give a pin for all the news of the world." "Now, now! don't go on so," said the fairy, "the princess is in the best of health; I have just seen her; and she is so beautiful, so very beautiful, that she can be a queen if she likes." And she told her the story from one end to the other, the queen weeping for joy to know that her daughter was so beautiful; and for sadness to think that she kept turkeys. "When we were great sovereigns in our kingdom," she said, "and lived in such magnificence, my poor husband and myself, we never could have believed that our child would one day keep turkeys." "It is that cruel Cancaline," said the fairy, "who, knowing how I love you, just to spite me, has reduced her to that condition; but she will come out of it, or I shall burn my books." "I do not wish her to marry the wicked king's son," said the queen. "Therefore, let us set out to-morrow to fetch her, and bring her here."

Now it happened that the wicked king's son, being very angry against Joliette, went and sat under a tree, and wept and howled aloud. His father, hearing him, went to the window and called out to him: "What are you crying for? What a fool you are!" "Because your turkey-herd will not love me," he answered. "What! she will not love you?" said the wicked king. "I insist on her loving you, or else she dies!" He called for his men-at-arms, and said to them: "Go and fetch her, for I shall punish her so that she will be sorry for her obstinacy." They went to the poultry-yard, and found Joliette in a beautiful dress of white satin, embroidered with gold, red and diamonds, and more than a thousand yards of ribbon. Never, never, in the wide world was seen such a lovely damsel. They hardly dared speak to her, thinking she must be a princess. "I beg of you, tell me whom you are looking for here," she asked. "Madam," they answered, "we are looking for a miserable little girl called Joliette." "Alas!" she said, "I am Joliette. What do you want of me?" They took hold of her in haste, bound her feet and her hands with thick cords for fear she might run away, and in this fashion they took her to the wicked king, who was with his son. When he saw that she was so lovely, he could not help being somewhat touched, and there is no doubt he would have taken pity on her, had he not been the wickedest and the cruellest man in the world. "Ah ha! you little good-for-nothing, you little toad, so you will not love my son? He is a hundred times handsomer than you, and one of his looks is worth more than the whole of your person. Come here, love him at once, or I will have you flayed." The princess, shaking like a little pigeon, knelt before him, saying: "Sire, I beg of you not to flay me. That would hurt me too much. Leave me one or two days to think what I ought to do, and then you

may do what you will with me." His son, who was desperate, wished her to be flayed, but they decided between them to shut her up in a tower, where she would not even see the sun.

Just then the good fairy came in the flying car with the queen. When they learnt all the news, the queen began to weep bitterly, saying she was ever unfortunate, and that she would rather her daughter were dead than that she should marry the wicked king's son. But the fairy said: "Take heart, I am going to tire them out so that you will be fully satisfied and revenged."

When the wicked king was going to bed the fairy turned herself into a little mouse, and hid under his pillow. As soon as he tried to fall asleep, she bit his ear. Very angry, he turned on his other side, and then she bit his other ear. "Murder!" he cried, and called for his attendants. When they came they found his two ears bitten and bleeding so freely that they could not stop the blood. While they were looking everywhere for the mouse, she did the same thing to the wicked king's son, who called his valets and showed them his ears all bitten, and had plasters put on them. The little mouse went back to the wicked king's room, who was now somewhat drowsy. She bit his nose and began to gnaw it. He put his hands up, but she bit and scratched them. He cried out: "Have mercy, I am lost!" Then she went into his mouth and nibbled at his tongue, his lips, his cheeks. His servants came and saw him in a fearful condition, hardly able to speak, so wounded was his tongue. He signed to them that a mouse had done it, and they looked in the mattress, the bolster, in every little corner. But she was not there, having gone to treat the son still worse, eating up his good eye, and he had but one. Rising like a madman with his sword in his hand, he rushed, blind as he was, to his father's room, who also had taken his sword, and who was storming and swearing that he would kill everybody if they did not catch the mouse. When he saw his son so desperate he burst out into abuse of him, and the son, who was in a burning rage, not recognising his father's voice, threw himself on him. The wicked king in wrath gave him a great blow with his sword, and

received one in return. Both fell in a great pool of blood. All their subjects, who hated them mortally, and who only served them out of fear, no longer having cause to be afraid of them, fastened cords to their feet and dragged them to the river, saying they were very happy to be rid of them.

And now the wicked king was dead and his son too. The good fairy, who knew this, fetched the queen, and they went together to the black tower where Joliette was imprisoned under forty locks. At three raps of the fairy's hazel wand the great door opened, and so did the others. They found the poor princess very sad and very silent. The queen threw herself on her neck. "My dearest one," she said, "I am your mother, Queen Joyous," and she told her the story of her life. When Joliette heard such good news she nearly died of joy, and throwing herself at the queen's feet, she embraced her knees, bathed her hands with her tears, and kissed her a thousand times. She caressed the fairy tenderly, who had brought for her baskets full of priceless jewels, gold, diamonds, bracelets, pearls, and the portrait of King Joyous surrounded with precious stones, all of which she placed before her. But the fairy said: "This is not a time for play. We must carry out a great revolution in the state. Let us go and speak to the people in the great hall of the castle."

She went first with a grave and serious face, the train of her dress sweeping more than ten ells behind her. The queen's dress of blue velvet, embroidered with gold, had a longer train still, for they had taken their finest clothes with them. Then they had crowns on their heads which shone like suns. Princess Joliette followed them, beautiful and modest, a perfect wonder to see. They bowed to all they met on the way, to the poor as well as the great, and all the people followed them, very eager to know who these fair ladies might be. When the hall was quite full, the good fairy said to the subjects of the wicked king that she wished to give them for a queen the daughter of King Joyous, whom they saw before them, that they would be happy under her rule, that if they would accept her she promised to seek a husband for her as perfect as herself, who would be always merry, and who would chase away sadness from every heart. At these words they all cried: "Yes, yes; we will! Too long have we been sad and miserable." And at that moment a hundred kinds of instruments struck up on all sides. Every one took his neighbour's hand and they danced in rings, singing round the queen and her daughter and the good fairy: "Yes, yes; we will."

Such was their welcome, and never was joy like theirs. Tables were spread, and they feasted and drank, and then went to bed to sleep soundly. When the young princess woke, the fairy presented to her the handsomest prince that ever saw the light. She had been to fetch him in the flying car from the other end of the world. He was as lovely as Joliette, and as soon as she saw him she loved him. As for him, he was charmed with the princess, and the queen was beside herself with joy. A feast and the most splendid garments were got ready, and the wedding was celebrated with endless merrymaking.

Charlotte Cinders

THERE was once upon a time a king and a queen who managed their affairs very badly. They were driven out of their kingdom, and had to sell first their crowns, then their clothes, their linen, their laces, their furniture, bit by bit, in order that they might have bread to eat. The pawnbrokers were tired of buying, for every day something new was sold. When at last they were stripped of nearly everything they possessed, the king said to his wife: "Here we are exiled from our kingdom, with nothing left us to live on. We must therefore earn our own and our poor children's bread. Think, then, what we shall do, for till now I have only followed kingcraft, which is very easy." The queen, who was very clever, asked eight days to think about the matter. At the end of that time, she said: "There is no reason why we should be miserable, your majesty. All you have to do is to make nets to catch birds in the woods and fish in the sea. While the lines are wearing out I shall make others for you. As for our three daughters, they are lazy minxes, and no mistake, who think they are still great ladies, and play at being such. They must be sent away, so far away that they will never come back; for it would be impossible for us to give them the fine clothes they would desire."

The king began to weep when he saw he must part from his children, for he was a kind father; but the queen was mistress. He agreed, therefore, to all her proposals, and said: "To-morrow morning rise early, and take your three daughters wherever you think suitable." As they were planning this, Princess Charlotte, the youngest girl, was listening through the keyhole. When she had found out the intention of her father and mother, she ran off as fast as ever she could to a large grotto, a long way from home, where the Fairy Merluche, her god-mother lived.

Charlotte took with her two pounds of fresh butter, some eggs, milk, and some flour to make a nice cake for her god-mother, so that she might get a good welcome from her. Very merrily did she set out on her journey, but the farther she went the more tired she grew. The soles of her shoes were quite worn through, and her pretty little feet were so torn that it was pitiful to see them. At last she had to give up, and sitting down on the grass, she began to cry.

A beautiful Spanish jennet passed by, saddled and bridled, with more diamonds on its saddle-cloth than would buy three whole towns. On seeing the princess, it began feeding quietly by her side, and bending its knee, it seemed to bow before her. "Pretty one," she said, taking hold of the bridle, "will you carry me to my god-mother, the fairy? I shall be so grateful if you will, for I am so tired that I am like to die. And if you help me now, I will give you nice oats, and hay, and fresh straw to lie on." The horse bent down almost to the ground before her, and little Charlotte jumped on its back, whereupon it set off running as lightly as a bird. At the entrance of the grotto, it stopped as if it had known the way, as indeed it did; for it was Merluche, knowing that her god-daughter was coming to see her, who had sent this beautiful horse.

When she was inside, she made three low bows to her god-mother, and taking the hem of her dress, she kissed it, saying: "Good-day, god-mother, how are you? Here is some butter, some milk, some flour, and some eggs, which I have brought to make a nice cake for you, just as we do at home." "Welcome, Charlotte," said the fairy; "come till I give you a kiss." So saying, she kissed her twice, which made Charlotte very happy, for Madam Merluche was not a common fairy. "Now, god-daughter," said she, "I want you to be my little maid. Take down my hair and comb it." The princess undid it, and combed it, in the cleverest possible way. "I know quite well," said Merluche, "why you came here. You overheard the king and the queen, who want to lead you away and lose you, and you wish that no such evil thing may happen to you. Well, you have only to take this ball of thread. It will never break. Fasten one end to the door of your house, and keep it in your hand. When the queen has left you, it will be easy to return by following the thread."

The princess thanked her god-mother, who filled a bag for her with beautiful dresses all of gold and silver, and after kissing her, mounted her again on the beautiful horse, and in two or three minutes she was landed at the door of their majesties' hut. "My little friend," said Charlotte to the horse, "you are very pretty, and very good, and you run faster than the sun. I thank you for your trouble, and now go back to where you came from." She entered the house very quietly and, hiding her bag under her pillow, went to her bed as if nothing had happened.

As soon as day dawned, the king woke his wife, saying: "Come, madam, come, get ready for the journey." She got up immediately, put on her thick shoes, a short skirt, a white camisole, and took a stick in her hand. Then she called her eldest daughter, whose name was Rose; her second, Amy; and her third, Sharp Ears, though she was usually called Charlotte. "I learnt in a dream last night," said the queen, "that we must go and see my sister. She will entertain us well, and we can eat and laugh as much as ever we like." Rose, who was miserable at living in this lonely place, said to her mother: "Very well, madam, let us go wherever you please. Provided that I get away from here, it doesn't matter to me." The two others said the same. So after bidding good-bye to the king, all the four set off. They went such a very long way that Sharp Ears began to be much afraid she would not have thread enough, for they had gone nearly a thousand leagues. She used always to walk behind her sisters, passing the thread deftly through the bushes. When the queen thought that her daughters would not be able to find their way back, she went into a large wood, and said: "My little lambs, go to sleep now. I shall be the shepherdess who watches round her flock, for fear the wolf should eat them." So lying down on the grass they fell asleep, and the queen left them there, thinking she should never see them again. Charlotte had shut her eyes, but was not asleep. "If I were a wicked girl," she said, "I should go away at once, leaving my sisters here to die, for they beat me and scratch me till the blood comes. But in spite of all their cruelty, I will not leave them." So she woke them, and told them the whole story. They began to cry, and begged her to take them along with her, and said they would give her lovely dolls, and their little silver dolls' house, and their other toys, and their sugar-plums. "I know well enough that you will do nothing of the kind," said Charlotte, "but all the same, I will be a kind sister to you." And getting up, she followed her trail of thread, and the princesses did so too, so that they got home almost as soon as the queen.

Stopping at the door, they heard the king saying: "My heart is very sore at seeing you coming back by yourself." "Well, but we didn't know what to do with our daughters," said the queen. "Yet, if you had brought my Charlotte back," replied the king, "I should not mind about the others, for they care for nobody." Tap, tap, came their knock. "Who is there?" said the king. "Your three daughters," they answered, "Rose, Amy, and Sharp Ears." The queen was all of a tremble. "Do not open the door," she said; "it must be their ghosts, for they themselves could not have come back." And the king, who was just as great a coward as his wife, said: "You are deceiving me; you are not my daughters." But Sharp Ears, who was quickwitted, said to him: "Father, I am going to bend down. Look at me through the cat's hole, and if I am not Charlotte, I'll let you beat me." The king looked as she had told him, and as soon as he recognised her, he opened the door to them. The queen pretended that she was very glad to see them, and told them she had forgotten something, and that she came to fetch it, but assuredly she would have found them again. And they made as if they believed her, and went up to their sleeping-place in a pretty little garret for the night.

"Well, sisters," said Charlotte, "you promised me a doll; give it me then." "And how can you expect it, you little monkey?" said they. "It is all on account of you that the king does not love us." Thereupon they took their distaffs and beat her without mercy. When they had chastised her well, she went to bed, but with so many scars and swellings that she could not sleep. So she heard the queen saying to the king: "I shall take them in another direction, still further off, and I am sure they will never return." When Charlotte heard this plan, she got up very quietly, meaning to pay another visit to her god-mother. Going into the poultry-house, she took two chickens and a fine cock, and wrung their necks, then two little rabbits that the queen was feeding up with cabbage against the next time they should be having a feast; and putting them all in a basket, she set off. But she had not gone a league, groping all the way, and in terror of her life, when the Spanish jennet galloped up to her, snorting and neighing. She thought it was all up with her, and that soldiers were coming to capture her, but when she saw the pretty horse all by itself, she mounted, delighted to go on her way in this comfortable fashion; and very soon she was at her god-mother's house.

After the usual greetings, she gave her the chickens, the cock, and the rabbits. Then she begged Merluche to help her by good counsel, making known to her how the queen had sworn to take them away to the end of the world. Merluche told the girl not to be miserable, and giving her a sack full of ashes, she said: "You will carry the bag in front of you, and shake it as you go. You will walk on the ashes, and when you want to return, you need only look for your footprints. But do not bring your sisters back. They are too wicked, and if you bring them, I will never see you any more." Charlotte took leave of her, taking with her by Merluche's orders some thirty or forty millions of diamonds in a little box which she put in her pocket. The horse was quite ready, and carried her off as before.

When day broke the queen called the princesses, and when they came she said to them: "The king is not very well. Last night I dreamt that I must go and gather flowers and herbs in a certain country where they are very good. They will make him young again; therefore let us set out at once." Rose and Amy, who could not believe their mother was anxious to get rid of them, were very sorry to hear this. However they had to set off; and they went so far that never was such a long journey made before. Charlotte, who did not say a word all the while, kept behind the others, shaking the ashes very cleverly, not letting the wind or the rain spoil any of them.

The queen, fully persuaded they could never find the way again, noticed one evening that her three daughters were fast asleep, so she took advantage of this to leave them and return home. When daylight came, and Charlotte knew that her mother

was no longer with them, she awoke her sisters. "We are alone," she said; "the queen has gone away." Rose and Amy began to cry, to tear their hair, and to beat their faces with their fists, "Alas!" they exclaimed; "what shall we do?" Charlotte was the kindest girl in the whole world, and again she took pity on her sisters. "Think what risk I am running," she said; "for when my god-mother gave me the means of returning, she forbade me to tell you the way, and said if I disobeyed her she would never see me again." Amy threw herself on Charlotte's neck, and so did Rose, thanking her so tenderly that before long they all three returned together to the king and the queen.

Their majesties were very much astonished at seeing the princesses again, and spoke of it all night long. And the youngest girl, who was not called Sharp Ears for nothing, heard them making up a fresh plot for the queen on the morrow to take them again into the wilds. She ran and woke her sisters. "Alas!" she said to them, "we are lost. The queen is determined to take us to some desert and leave us there. It is your fault that my god-mother is angry, and that I dare not go and find her as I always did before." They were very much troubled, and one said to the other: "What shall we do, my sister, what shall we do?" At last Amy said to the others: "There is no need to distress ourselves. Old Merluche hasn't the whole stock of cleverness in the world. We need only take peas with us and sow them along the road, and by the traces of their growth we can come back." Rose thought this a capital plan, so they took a large quantity of peas, and filled their pockets. But Sharp Ears, instead of carrying peas, took the bag with the pretty clothes, and the little box of diamonds, and as soon as the queen called them to be off, they were quite ready.

"I dreamt last night," she said to them, "that in a country which I need not name there are three handsome princes waiting to marry you. I am going to take you there to see if my dream is true." The queen walked on in front, and her daughters after her, sowing their peas, and quite easy in their minds, having no doubt but that they would return home again. This time the queen travelled farther than she had ever done before; but one dark night she left them, and came back to the king. Very tired was she when she reached home, but very glad not to have the cares of such a large household on her shoulders.

The three princesses, after sleeping till eleven o'clock in the morning, woke up. It was Charlotte who first perceived the queen's absence, and though she expected it, she could not help crying, having, so far as getting back was concerned, more confidence in her god-mother's help than in her sisters' cleverness. In a great fright, she told them the queen had gone, and that they must follow her as soon as possible. "Hold your tongue, you little monkey," said Rose; "we'll be able to find the road whenever we like. We don't want you to interfere unless your opinion is asked." Charlotte did not dare to answer, but when they tried to find the way, not a mark or a footpath could be found. The pigeons, of which there are a great number in that country, had eaten up the peas, and so the princesses began to cry and howl. After being two days without food, Rose said to Amy: "Sister, have you nothing to eat?" "No," she answered. She asked Charlotte the same thing. "No more have I," she replied, "but I have just found an acorn." "Ah! give it to me," said one. "Give it to me," said the other; and each of them wanted to have it. "One acorn would hardly satisfy three of us," said Charlotte; "let us plant it; another will grow out of it for our use." They agreed, though there seemed little likelihood that a tree would grow in a country where there were none, and where only cabbages and lettuces were to be seen. The princesses ate of these, and if they had been very delicate, they would have died a hundred times. Nearly every night they lay down under the stars, and every morning and every evening went in turns to water the acorn, saying: " Grow, grow, pretty acorn!" And it began to grow visibly. When it had grown to some height, Rose wished to climb up on it, but it was not strong enough to bear her, and feeling it bend under her weight, she got down. The same thing happened to Amy. Charlotte, lighter than the others, stopped longer, and they asked her: "Do you see nothing, sister?" "No, I see nothing," she answered. "That is because the oak is not high enough," said Rose; so they went on watering it, and saying: "Grow, grow, pretty acorn!" Charlotte never failed to climb up twice a day, and one morning when she was there Amy said to Rose: "I have found a bag our sister has hidden. What can be in it?" Rose said Charlotte had told her it was old lace she was mending. "Well, I think there are sugar-plums in it," said Amy. She was greedy, and wanted to see what was in it. She did find the laces of the king and the queen, but they served to hide Charlotte's beautiful clothes and the box of diamonds. "Well, was there ever such a wicked little creature?" she cried. "Let us take them all and

put stones in their place." This they did without delay. When Charlotte came back, she did not notice what her sisters had done, for she did not think of ornaments in a desert. Her one thought was of the oak, which was growing to be the finest ever seen.

One time when she had climbed up and her sisters as usual asked her if she saw nothing, "I see," she cried, "a large house, so beautiful—so very, very beautiful, that I cannot describe it to you. The walls are of emeralds and rubies, the roof of diamonds, and it is all covered with golden bells; the weathercocks turn and turn with the wind." "That is not true," they said; "it is not so beautiful as you say." "Believe me, it is," replied Charlotte; "I don't tell lies. Come and see for yourselves, for my eyes are quite dazzled." Rose climbed up into the tree, and when she saw the castle, she could speak of nothing else. Amy, who was very curious, would not be behind-hand, and climbing up she was just as delighted as her sisters. "Certainly," they said, "we must go to that palace; perhaps we shall find handsome princes there who will only be too happy to marry us." All the evening long they spoke of nothing but their plan. Then they lay down on the grass, and when Charlotte seemed to be asleep, Rose said to Amy: "Do you know what we must do, sister? Get up and let us dress ourselves in the rich dresses Charlotte has brought." "You are right," said Amy; so they got up, curled their hair, powdered their faces, stuck on beauty spots, and dressed themselves in gold and silver gowns, all covered with diamonds. Never was seen such a magnificent sight.

Charlotte, not knowing that her wicked sisters had robbed her, took her bag with the intention of dressing, and she was in great distress at only finding pebbles. At the same time she saw her sisters decked out like suns. She wept, and reproached them with their breach of faith to her, but they only laughed and mocked at her. "Would you really dare," she said, "to take me to the castle without any pretty dresses or ornaments at all?" "We have not too many for ourselves," replied Rose, "and will beat you if you talk any more about it." "But," Charlotte went on, "these dresses are mine. My god-mother gave me them. You have no part in them." "If you speak another word," they said, "we shall kill you, and bury you, and nobody will know anything about it." And poor Charlotte, afraid to anger them, followed them quietly, walking some steps behind, just as if she were their servant.

The nearer they came to the house, the more wonderful it seemed. "Hi!" said Rose and Amy, "what a good time we are going to have! What good cheer we shall partake of as we sit at the king's table. But as for Charlotte, she will wash the dishes in the kitchen, for she is just like a scullion, and if any one asks who she is, let us take care not to call her our sister, but rather the little village herd." Charlotte, who was full of intelligence, and very pretty, was in great distress at such ill-treatment. When they went up to the gate of the castle they knocked, and at once a hideous old woman came to open the door to them. She had only one eye, in the middle of her forehead, but it was bigger than five or six ordinary eyes; her nose was flat, her complexion dark, and her mouth was so horrible that it made every one afraid to look at it; she was fifteen feet high, and thirty in girth. "Oh, you miserable girls," she said, " what brings you here? Do you not know that this is the ogre's castle, and that all of you together would hardly be enough for his breakfast? But I am better than my husband. Come in, I shall not eat you up all at once. You may have the comfort of living two or three days more." When they heard the ogress speaking in this fashion, they ran away, thinking they could escape, but one of her strides was as good as fifty of theirs, and running after them, she caught them by their hair or by the skin of their necks. Bundling them under her arm, she threw all three of them into the cellar, which was full of toads and adders, and where you walked on the bones of those that had already been eaten.

As she wanted to crunch up Charlotte on the spot she ran to fetch vinegar and salt to eat her as a salad, but hearing the ogre coming, and thinking the princesses' skin white and delicate, she made up her mind to eat them all by herself. So she hastily put them into a large tub where they could only see out through a hole.

The ogre was six times as tall as his wife. When he spoke the house shook: when he coughed you would have thought it was claps of thunder. He had only one eye, a large, ugly one, his hair stood all on end, and he leant on a log which he used for a stick. In his hand he held a covered basket out of which he drew fifteen little children that he had stolen on the road, and whom he swallowed as if they had been fifteen fresh eggs. When the three princesses saw him, they shook with terror under the tub, and dared no longer cry aloud for fear he should hear them. But low to themselves they said: "He'll eat us all alive; how can we escape?" The ogre said to his wife: "I smell fresh meat, give me some." "Indeed," said the ogress, "you always think you smell fresh meat. It is four sheep that passed by." "Oh, I make no mistake," said the ogre. "I smell fresh meat for certain. I am going to look everywhere for it." "Look for it, then," she said, "but you won't find any." "If I find it," answered the ogre, "and if you are hiding it, I shall cut off your head to make me a ball." In terror at this threat she said to him: "Don't be angry, my little ogre, I am going to tell you the truth. To-day there came here three young maidens whom I kept, but it would be a pity to eat them, for they know how to do everything. As I am now old I need rest; our beautiful house, as you see, is in very bad order; our bread is not baked properly; our soup no longer tastes good to you, and I don't look so beautiful in your eyes since I have been killing myself with work. They will, therefore, be my servants, so I beg of you not to eat them just now. If you wish to at some future time you can do as you like."

The ogre found it very hard to promise not to eat them up at once. "Let me have my own way," he said; "I shall only eat two of them." "No, you shall not eat any of them." "Very well; I shall only eat the little one." But she answered: "No, you shall not eat one of them." At last, after quarreling for a long time, he promised not to eat them; while the ogress thought to herself: "When he goes to the hunt I shall eat them and tell him they have run away."

The ogre came out of the cellar and ordered them to be brought before him. The poor girls were nearly dead with fright; but the ogress reassured them. When he saw them he asked them what they could do, and they told him they could sweep and sew and spin perfectly; that their stews were so delicious that you would like to eat the plate even on which they were served; and as for their bread, cakes, and pies—why, people came for them from a thousand miles a round. The ogre was greedy, and so he said: "Now, then, set these fine cooks to work at once." "But," said he, turning to Charlotte, "when you have lit the fire, how can you tell if the oven be hot enough?" "My lord," she answered, "I throw butter in, and then I taste it with my tongue." "Very well," he said, "light the fire then." The oven was as big as a stable, for the ogre and ogress ate more bread than two armies. The princess made an enormous fire, which blazed like a furnace; and the ogre, who was standing by, ate a hundred lambs and a hundred suckling pigs while waiting for the new bread. Rose and Amy kneaded the dough. "Well," said the great ogre, "is the oven hot?" "My lord," replied Charlote, "you will see presently." And so saying she threw a thousand pounds of butter into the oven. "I should try it with my tongue," she said, "but I am too little." "I am big enough," said the ogre, and bending down he went so far into the oven that he could not draw back again, so that he was burned to the bones. When the ogress came to the oven she was mightily astonished to find a mountain of cinders instead of her husband.

Rose and Amy, who saw that she was in great distress, comforted her as they could, but they feared lest her grief should be consoled only too soon, and that regaining her appetite she would put them in a salad, as she had meant to do before. So they said to her: "Take courage, madam; you will find some king or some marquis who will be happy to marry you." At that she smiled a little, showing her teeth, which were longer than your finger. When they saw she was in a good humour, Charlotte said: "If you would but leave off wearing those horrible bear-skins, and dress

a little more fashionably! We could arrange your hair beautifully, and you would be like a star." "Come then," she said, "let us see what you can do; but be sure that if I find any ladies more beautiful than myself I shall hack you into little bits." Thereupon the three princesses took off her cap, and began to comb and curl her hair, entertaining her all the while with their chatter. Then Charlotte took a hatchet, and with a great blow from behind, severed her head from her body.

Never was there such joy. They climbed up to the roof of the house to amuse themselves by ringing the golden bells; they ran through all the rooms, which were of pearls and diamonds, and furnished so richly that they nearly died of joy. They laughed, they sang. Nothing was lacking. They had wheat, and sweetmeat, fruits, and dolls, as many as they liked. Rose and Amy slept in beds hung with brocade and velvet, and they said to each other: "Here we are richer than was our father in his kingdom, but we want husbands. No one will come here, for this house is certainly looked on as a death-trap, and nobody knows of the death of the ogre and his wife. We must go to the nearest town to show ourselves off in our fine clothes, and it will not be long before we find honest merchants who will be glad enough to wed with princesses." As soon as they were dressed they told Charlotte that they were going for a walk, and that she must stop at home to look after the house and the washing, so that when they came back everything might be neat and clean; that if it were not they would beat her soundly. Poor Charlotte, stricken with grief, stopped alone in the house, sweeping, cleaning, washing, without a moment's rest, and always crying. "How unhappy I am," she said "to have disobeyed my god-mother! All kinds of evils happen to me. My sisters have stolen my beautiful clothes to dress themselves in. Without me the ogre and his wife would still be alive and well; and of what benefit is it to me that I killed them? It would have been as good to have been eaten by them as to live as I live now." When she had said this she was almost choked with her tears. Then her sisters came back, loaded with Portuguese oranges, preserves, and sugar, saying to her: "Oh, what a fine ball we have been to! And what a crowd was there! The king's son was dancing; we had a great many attentions paid us. But come now, pull off our shoes, and wash us. That's all you are good for." Charlotte did as she was told, and if by any chance a word of complaint escaped her, they threw themselves on her, beating her till she was senseless.

Next day they went again, and returned to tell of all the wonders they had seen. One evening, when Charlotte was sitting near the fire on a little heap of cinders, for want of anything else to do, she peered into the crevices of the chimney, and as she looked she found a little key, so old, and so rusty, that it gave her a great deal of trouble to clean it. When it was polished, she found it was gold, and she thought that a golden key must be for opening some beautiful little chest. So she began to run through the whole house, trying the key in all the locks, till at last she found it fitted a casket of perfect workmanship. Opening this, she found in it dresses, diamonds, lace, linen, and very costly ribbons. She said nothing about her good fortune to her sisters, but waited impatiently till they should go out next day, and as soon as they had gone out of her sight, she dressed herself in such a way that she was more beautiful than the sun or the moon.

Thus decked out, she went to the same ball where her sisters were dancing, and though she wore no mask, she was so changed for the better that they did not recognise her. As soon as she made her appearance in the assembly a murmur of voices arose, some expessing their admiration, some their jealousy. She was asked to dance, and she excelled all the ladies in that as she did in beauty. The mistress of the house coming up to her and making her a deep bow, begged to know what she was called, so that she might ever keep in remembrance the name of so distinguished a lady. With much courtesy she answered that she was called Cinders. Not a lover was there but forgot his mistress for Cinders: not a poet but made verses to her. Never did a name make such a sensation in such a short time, and the echoes brought nothing back but Cinders's praises. No one had eyes enough to look on her, or voice enough to sing her praises.

Rose and Amy, who at first had made a great noise wherever they appeared, now seeing the reception given to the new-comer, were bursting with rage. But Charlotte kept clear of all their spite with the most perfect grace possible. To look at her you would have said she was born to rule, and Rose and Amy who never saw their sister but with soot on her face and grimier-looking than a little dog, had so forgotten all about her beauty that they did not recognise her at all, and paid court to Cinders like the others. As soon as the ball was nearly over she set off quickly, reached home, undressed in haste, and put on her rags again. When her sisters

came back they said: "Ah! Charlotte, we have just been seeing a young princess who is quite charming. She is not an ugly ape like you. She is white as snow, and redder than roses. Her teeth are of pearl and her lips of coral. Her dress must weigh more than a thousand pounds, for it is all of gold and diamonds. Ah, how beautiful! how lovely she is!" And Charlotte would answer between her teeth: "I was like that, I was like that." "What are you muttering?" they said. And Charlotte answered still lower: "I was like that." This little entertainment lasted for a long time. Hardly a day passed but Charlotte put on new clothes, for it was a fairy casket, and the more you took from it, the more was in it, and the clothes that came out of it were so fashionable that ladies took her for their model.

One evening when Charlotte had danced more than usual, and had stopped rather late, in her desire to make up for lost time and to get home before her sisters, she walked as fast as ever she could, and let fall one of her slippers, which was of red velvet embroidered with pearls. She did all she could to find it again on the road, but the night was so dark that her trouble was in vain, and she had to go in with only one foot shod.

Next day, Prince James, the eldest son of the king, on his way to the chase, found Charlotte's slipper. He ordered them to pick it up, looked at it, turned it this way and that, kissed it, cherished it, and bore it away with him. From that day he would not eat. He grew thin and changed, was as yellow as a quince, melancholy, and spiritless. The king and queen, who loved him to distraction, sent in all directions for fine game and preserves for him. But to him these seemed less than nothing, and he only looked at them all, and would not answer the queen when she spoke to him. They sent to fetch doctors from all parts, even from Paris and Montpellier. When they arrived they were shown the prince, and having watched him three days and three nights without once leaving him, they came to the conclusion that he was in love, and that he would die if a remedy were not provided.

The queen, who loved him tenderly, wept oceans of tears because she could not find out whom he loved and so arrange for his marriage. She brought the most beautiful ladies to his room, but he would not even look at them. At last she said to him one day: "My dear son, you will kill us with grief, for you are in love, and you hide your feelings from us. Tell us whom it is you long for, and she shall be yours even were she but a simple shepherdess." The prince, assured by the queen's promises, drew the slipper out from below his pillow, and showed it to her. "Madam," he said, "this is the cause of my illness. I found this dear little pretty slipper when I was going to the chase, and I shall never marry any but the lady whom it fits." "Very well, my son," said the queen, "do not grieve, we will send in search of her." And she went to tell the news to the king, who was very much astonished. Without delay he ordered that an announcement should be made with drums and trumpets that all the girls and all the women should come and try on the slipper, and that whosoever it should fit should wed with the prince. When all the ladies had heard the announcement they washed their feet with all sorts of waters, pastes, and pomades. There were some who peeled their feet, so that the skin should be more beautiful, others pared them, or fasted, to make them smaller. In crowds they set out to try on the slipper, but not one would it fit, and the more unavailing attempts were made the greater was the prince's distress.

Rose and Amy one day dressed themselves so fine that they were a wonder to see. "Where are you going?" said Charlotte. "We are going to the great city," they answered, "where the king and the queen dwell, to try on the slipper which the king's son found; for if it fits one of us, the prince will marry her and she shall be a queen." "And might I go too?" said Charlotte. "You, in truth!" said they. "You are a silly little goose. Be off and water the cabbages, you good-for-nothing."

Charlotte at once thought of putting on her finest clothes to go and try her luck with the others, for she had some idea that she would have a good chance. But what troubled her was that she did not know the way, for the ball they had danced at was not in the great town. She dressed in all her splendour, in a gown of blue satin covered with stars of diamonds, a sun made of them on her head, a full moon on her back, and all shining so brilliantly that you could not look at her without flinching. When she opened the door to go out she was very much astonished to find the beautiful Spanish jennet that had carried her to her god-mother. She caressed him, saying: "Welcome, little one; for you I am obliged to my god-mother, Merluche." Then it bent down, and she rode on it like a nymph. It was all covered with golden bells and ribbons, and its saddle cloth and bridle were priceless. As for Charlotte, she was far more beautiful than the fair Helen.

The jennet trotted lightly along to the music of the bells, cling, cling, cling. Rose and Amy hearing the sound, turned and saw her coming. But what was their surprise at that moment, when they recognised that it was Charlotte Cinders! They themselves were all draggled, and their fine clothes covered with mud. "Sister," said Rose to Amy, "I declare to you that that is Charlote Cinders." The other said the same; and Charlotte passing close by at the moment, they were bespattered by her horse's hoofs, and their faces splashed with mud. And Charlotte laughed as she said: "Your highnesses, Cinderella despises you as much as you deserve;" then riding past them like an arrow she was gone. Amy and Rose looked at each other. "Are we dreaming?" they said. "Who could have given Charlotte her fine clothes and the horse? What an astonishing thing! She is in luck. She will put the slipper on, and our journey will be in vain."

While they were mourning over their disappointment, Charlotte reached the palace, and as soon as she came in sight, every one thought she was a queen. The soldiers presented arms, the drums began to beat, the trumpets sounded, and all the doors were flung open. Those who had seen her at the ball ran in front of her, calling out: "Room, make room for Cinders, the wonder of the

world!" With such pomp, she entered the dying prince's room, who, casting his eyes on her, was enchanted, and full of desire that her foot might be small enough to fit the slipper. Without delay, she put it on, and showed the other one which she had brought on purpose. "Long live Prince James!" they burst out. "Long live the princess who will be our queen!" The prince rose from his bed, and came forward to kiss her hands, and she thought him handsome and full of wit as he poured his compliments upon her. The king and queen, who had been told the news, hastened to the spot, and the queen, taking Charlotte in her arms, called her her daughter, her darling, her little queen. She gave her beautiful gifts, and the generous king added more. The cannons were fired, there was music of violins, and of pipes, and all kinds of instruments, and nothing was heard but the sounds of dancing and merriment.

The king, the queen, and the prince begged Cinders to give her consent to the marriage. "No," she said, "I must first of all tell you my story," which she did very shortly. When they heard that she was born a princess, they were still more delighted, and almost beside themselves with joy. But when she told them the names of the king and queen, her father and mother, they knew that it was they themselves who had conquered their kingdom, and told her so. Then she swore she would not consent to the marriage till they gave back her father's estates. This they promised, for having more than a hundred kingdoms, one more or less was of very little consequence.

In the meanwhile Amy and Rose arrived, and the first news they heard was that Cinders had put on the slipper. They did not know what to say or to do, and would have liked to have gone back without seeing her, but when she heard they were come, she ordered them to appear before her, and instead of scowling at them, and of punishing them as they deserved, she rose and came forward to embrace them tenderly. Then presenting them to the queen, she said: "Madam, these are my sisters, who are very amiable; I beg that you will love them." So astounded were they at

Charlotte's goodness, that they could not utter a word. She promised them that they should return to their own kingdom, which the prince wished to restore to their family. At these words they threw themselves on their knees before her weeping for joy.

Never was there such a wedding-feast. Charlotte wrote to her god-mother, and put her letter along with magnificent gifts on the beautiful jennet. In the letter she begged her to find the king and queen, to tell them of her good fortune, and to say they might return to their kingdom when they liked. Merluche, the fairy, carried out these instructions perfectly, and Charlotte's father and mother went back to their own estates, and her sisters became queens like herself.

ONCE upon a time there was a poor labourer who, knowing he was about to die, wished to leave nothing behind him that his son and daughter could quarrel about after his death, for he loved them tenderly. "Your mother brought me for a dowry," he said, "two stools and a straw mattress. These, with my hen, would have been my only belongings, had not a pot of pinks and a silver ring been given me by a great lady who lived for some time in my poor cottage. When she went away, she said to me: 'My good man, here is a present for you. Be careful to water the pinks, and to keep the ring in a safe place. I may also tell you that your daughter will be wonderfully beautiful. Call her Felicity, and give her the ring and the pinks to comfort her for being so poor.' So, dear Felicity," the good man went on, "you shall have both these, and the rest of my belongings I leave to your brother."

The labourer's two children appeared to be satisfied. Their father died, and they wept, and afterwards they shared his belongings without any dispute. Felicity thought her brother loved her, but once when she was about to sit down on one of the stools, he said to her in an angry tone: "You keep your pinks and your ring, but don't meddle with my stool. I like order in my house." Felicity, who was very gentle, began to cry quietly, and remained standing, while John (that was the brother's name) sat there as fine as if he had been a learned doctor. Supper time came on, John had a beautiful, fresh egg which his only hen had laid, and he threw the shell towards his sister, saying: "See, I have nothing else to give you; if that isn't enough, go and hunt for frogs; there are plenty in the marsh nearby." Felicity answered nothing, but lifting her eyes to heaven she wept again; then she went to her own room. She found it filled with a delicious scent, which she knew, of course, must be from her pinks. She went up to them, saying, in a sad voice: "Pretty pinks, with all your different colours so fair to see, how you comfort my sad heart by your sweet scent. Never fear that I shall let you want for water, or with cruel hand wrench you from your stalks. I shall take care of you, for you are all I have in the world." Then she looked to see if they wanted watering. They were very dry, so she took the pitcher and ran out in the moonlight to the stream some little way off. As she had walked very fast, she sat down on the bank to rest, but hardly had she done so before she saw a lady, whose majestic air beseemed the large number of attendants who accompanied her. Six maids-of-honour held up the train of her robe, while she leaned on two others. Her guards marched before her, richly clad in amaranth velvet embroidered with pearls. They carried an armchair spread with cloth of gold, on which she presently sat down, and a portable canopy was quickly set up over her head. At the same time there were others spreading a table all covered with golden vessels and crystal vases. An excellent supper was served on the banks of the stream, and the soft murmur of the water seemed to blend with the different voices that were singing these words:

"Soft and low the summer air
Gently stirs the woodlands there;
Bright flowers glittering on the sod
Mark where Flora's feet have trod;
'Neath the cool shades hear the choirs
Of birds that sing their soft desires;
Would you catch the soft notes too?
Lovers plenty wait for you."

Felicity hid in a little corner, not daring to move, so surprised was she with all that was happening. After a moment the queen said to one of her squires: "It seems to me that I see a shepherdess near that bush. Bring her here." So Felicity came forward; and though she was naturally very timid, she did not fail to make a deep bow to the queen, and she did it with so much grace that those who saw her were much astonished. Taking the hem of the queen's robe in her hand she kissed it, and then stood before her with her eyes cast down, the pink blush on her cheek showing up the whiteness of her complexion. Altogether you could not fail to see in her manners that air of mild simplicity that is so charming in young people. "What are you doing here?" the queen asked her. "Are you not afraid of robbers?" "Alas! madam," said Felicity, "I have only a cotton frock; so what good would it do them to rob a poor shepherdess like me?" "You are not rich then?" replied the queen, smiling. "I am so poor," said Felicity, "that my whole inheritance from my father is a pot of pinks and a silver ring." "But you have a heart," added the queen. "If some one wished to take it from you, would you give it away?" "I do not know what it means to give away my heart, madam," she replied. "I have always heard that without one's heart one cannot live; that when it is wounded one must die, and in spite of my poverty I am not sorry to live." "You will always be right, my pretty girl, to defend your heart. But tell me," the queen went on, "did you have a good supper this evening?" "No, madam," said Felicity, "my brother ate up everything." The queen ordered them to lay a place for her, and setting her down at the table, she gave her all the best things on it. The young shepherdess was so struck with admiration, and so touched with the queen's kindness, that she could hardly eat a morsel. "I would like very much to know," said the queen, "what you were doing so late at the stream." "Madam," she answered, "there is my pitcher; I was fetching water to water my pinks." So saying she bent down to take hold of the pitcher which was near her; but when she showed it to the queen she was much astonished to find it turned into a golden one, all covered with diamonds and filled with deliciously-scented water. She dared not take it away with her, fearing it was not her own. "I give it to you Felicity," said the queen. "Go and water the flowers which you take such good care of, and do not forget that the Queen of the Woods means to be a friend to you." At these words the shepherdess threw herself at her feet. "After giving you my very humble thanks, madam," she said, "for the honour you do me, I make so bold as to ask you to wait here a moment. I am going to fetch you the half of what belongs to me, my pot of pinks. It can never be in better hands than yours." "Very well, Felicity," said the queen, gently stroking her cheeks. "I will remain here till you return." Felicity took her golden pitcher, and ran to her little room; but while she had been away her brother John had gone in, taken away her pot of pinks, and put a big cabbage in its place. When Felicity saw this miserable cabbage she was in despair, and hesitated whether she should go back to the stream or not. At last she made up her mind to do so, and kneeling down before the queen she said: "Madam, John has stolen my pot of pinks; I have only my ring left, and I beg you to take it as a proof of my gratitude." "If I take your ring, pretty shepherdess," said the queen, "you will be ruined." "Ah! madam," she answered, with a pretty air of grace, "if I have your favour I cannot be ruined." The queen took Felicity's ring and put it on her finger. Then she got into her chariot of coral, decked with emeralds, which was drawn by six white horses, more splendid than the equipage of the sun. Felicity followed her with her eyes as long as she could, till the turns in the forest roads hid her from her sight. Then she went back to John, her mind full of this adventure.

The first thing she did on entering her room was to throw the cabbage out of the window. But she was much astonished to hear a voice crying: "Ah! you have killed me!" She could not understand what these cries could mean, for cabbages are not in the habit of talking. As soon as it was day, Felicity, anxious about her pot of pinks, went outside to look for it, and the first thing she found was the miserable cabbage. Giving it a kick, she said: "What are you doing here? Do you think you do as well in my room as my pinks?" "If I had not been put there," replied the cabbage, "I should never have thought of intruding." Felicity trembled, for she was very much afraid. But the cabbage spoke once more. "If you will only put me back amongst my kind, I will tell you in two words that your pinks are in John's bed." Felicity, in despair, did not know how to get possession of them, but she was kind enough first to plant the cabbage, and then taking up her brother's favourite hen, she said: "Naughty creature! I shall make you pay for all the trouble that John gives me." "Ah! shepherdess," said the hen, "let me live, and as I am of a very talkative humour, I shall tell you the most interesting things. Do you think that you are the daughter of the labourer in whose house you have grown up? No, fair Felicity, he was not your father. But the queen who gave you life had

already had six daughters, and—as if she could have borne a son if she had wished—her husband and her father-in-law told her they would stab her if she did not give them an heir. The poor queen, in great distress, was about to have another child. They shut her up in a castle, surrounded her with guards, or rather executioners, who were ordered to kill her if she bore another daughter. The princess, terrified at the danger that threatened her, neither ate nor slept. But she had a sister who was a fairy, and she wrote to tell her of her fears. The fairy, too, was to bear a child, whom she knew would be a son. When he was born, therefore, she packed her son comfortably in a basket, which she gave in charge to the winds, telling them to carry the little prince into the queen's room, and exchange him for the daughter whom she would bear. This plan was, however, of no use, for the queen, not receiving news from her sister the fairy, took advantage of the good nature of one of her guards, who pitied her and let her escape by a cord ladder. As soon as you were born, the poor queen, seeking a hiding-place, came to this hut half dead with fatigue and pain. I was an industrious woman," said the hen, "and a good nurse, so she gave you in charge to me, telling me all her sorrows, with which she was so overcome that she died before she had time to tell us what should be done with you. As I have been very fond of talking all my life, I could not keep from telling this adventure. So one day there came here a beautiful lady, to whom I related everything I knew about it. She touched me immediately with her wand, and I was turned into a hen, and never could speak any more. My grief was terrible, and my husband, who was from home when the change occurred, never knew the truth. When he came back he looked for me everywhere, till at last he thought I was drowned, or that the beasts of the forest had devoured me. The same lady who had done me such a wrong passed by here a second time; she ordered him to call you Felicity, and made him a present of a pot of pinks and a silver ring. But while she was in the hut, there came five-and-twenty of your royal father's guards, who were seeking

you with evil intentions. She muttered some words, and they were all turned into green cabbages, one of which it was you threw out of the window last night. I had never heard him speak till now. I myself could not speak either, and I know not how my voice has come back to me."

The princess was very much astonished at the wonders which the hen told her. She felt stirred with pity for her, and said: "I am deeply sorry, my poor nurse, that you were turned into a hen. I should very much like to give you back your former shape if I could. But despair of nothing. It seems to me that all the things you have just told me about cannot always remain as they are now. Meanwhile I am going to look for my pinks, for I love them better than anything else."

John had gone to the wood, never imagining that Felicity would think of rummaging in his bed. She was delighted that he was from home, and was hoping she would find no difficulty, when all at once she saw a great quantity of enormous rats ready for fight. They were drawn up in battalions, with the bed in question behind them, and the stools by their sides. Some large mice formed a reserve force, bent on fighting like Amazons. Felicity was much surprised, and dared not go nearer, for the rats were attacking her, biting her, and making the blood flow. "What!" she cried, "my pinks, my dear pinks, will you remain in such bad company?" All at once the thought struck her that perhaps the perfumed water which she kept in the golden pitcher might have some special virtue, so she ran to fetch it, and threw some drops of it on the host of rats and mice. In a moment the rabble scampered off, each one to his hole, while the princess bore away her beautiful pinks in haste. They were nearly dead, so much in want of water were they, and she poured on them all she had in her golden pitcher. She was smelling them with great delight when she heard a very sweet voice which came from amongst the leaves and which said: "Wonderful Felicity! Behold the happy day so longed for, when I may declare my feelings to you; for the power of your beauty is such, that even flowers are conscious of it." The princess, trembling and astonished at having heard a cabbage and a hen talk, and now a pot of pinks, and at having seen an army of rats, turned pale and fainted.

At that moment John arrived. His work and the heat of the sun had so excited him, that when he saw that Felicity had come to seek for her pinks, and had found them, he dragged her to the door and put her out. Hardly had her cheeks touched the cool earth before she opened her beautiful eyes, and saw standing by her the Queen of the Woods, ever charming and dignified. "You have a wicked brother." she said to Felicity, "I saw how cruelly he threw you out here. Do you wish to be revenged on him?" "No,

madam," she said, "I do not know what anger is, and his evil nature cannot change mine." "But," said the queen, "I have a strong conviction that this coarse labourer is not your brother; what do you think?" "All the facts that I am aware of go to prove that he is, madam," replied the shepherdess, modestly, "and I must believe them." "What!" said the queen, "Have you not heard that you were born a princess?" "I have just heard it," she answered; "yet dare I venture to boast of a thing of which I have no proof?" "Ah, dear child," said the queen, "how I like to see you in this humour! I know now that the obscure bringing up you have had has not stifled the noble blood in your veins. Yes, you are a princess, and it has not been in my power to save you from the misfortunes which you have experienced up till now."

Here she was interrupted by the arrival of a young man, who was fairer than the day. He was dressed in a long doublet of green and gold silk, fastened with large buttons of emeralds and rubies and diamonds. On his head was a crown of pinks, and his hair hung down over his shoulders. As soon as he saw the queen, he bent one knee to the ground and greeted her respectfully. "Ah! dear Pink," she said, "the unhappy term of your enchantment has come to an end thanks to fair Felicity. What joy to see you!" And she clasped him close in her arms, and then turning towards the shepherdess she said: "Fair princess, I know all that the hen has told you; but what you do not know is that the zephyrs, whom I had ordered to exchange my son for you, carried him to a flower-bed while they were searching for your mother, who was my sister. Meanwhile a fairy who knew the most secret things, and with whom I had long been on bad terms, so cleverly seized the opportunity she had been on the watch for ever since the birth of my son, that she changed him on the spot into a pot of pinks, and for all my skill I could not prevent this misfortune. Stung with grief, I used all my art to find a remedy, and I could think of nothing better than to bring Prince Pink to the place where you were being brought up, guessing that when you would have watered the flowers with the delicious water which I had in the golden vase, he would speak, he would love you, and that after that nothing would disturb your peace. I had even in my possession the silver ring which it was necessary for me to receive from your hand, as a sign that the hour was at hand when the charm should lose its force, in spite of the rats and the mice that our enemy sent out to hinder you from touching the pinks. So, dear Felicity, if my son marries you with this ring, your happiness will never end. Look now if the prince seems to you handsome enough to take him for a husband." "Madam," she replied, blushing, " you heap favours on me. I know that you are my aunt, that by your skill the guards sent to kill me were turned into cabbages, and my nurse into a hen. In proposing to marry me to Prince Pink, you do me more honour than I deserve. But, may I tell you why I hesitate? I do not know what his feelings are for me, and I begin to feel for the first time in my life that I would not be satisfied if he did not love me." "Have no doubts on that point, fair princess." said Pink; "For long you have impressed me as you wish to impress me now, and if I had been able to speak, what should I not have told you every day as to how my affection was growing, burning within me? But I am an unfortunate prince to whom you are quite indifferent." Then he repeated these verses to her:

"Ah! kinder was my lot before,
    When I, a flower, was all your care,
When on my blossoms you set store,
    And happier were that I was fair;
For your dear eyes I bloomed anew,
    For you I gathered perfume sweet;
And when I looked in vain for you
    While far off tarried your feet,
My faded petals told a tale
    Of a poor heart that down would sink,
And a poor life that' gan to fail.
    Then water cool you'd bid me drink,

And kisses sweet would be my food,
And I was whole and bloomed again,
My soul aglow with gratitude;
To prove my passion I was fain;
Oh! how I longed some fairy power
Would break the charm that bound so fast
My being in a fragile flower!
My prayers are answered now at last.
I see you, love you, and can speak
My love, and all my soul's desire—
Only, alas! in vain I seek
What once was mine. Your looks retire,
Your words their former feeling lack.
Gods! did I of my lot complain?
My human shape I give you back
Ah, let me be a flower again!"

The princess seemed very pleased with Pink's gallantry, and praised highly the verses he had made on the spot, and though she was not used to hearing verses, she spoke of them like a person of good taste. The queen, who was impatient at seeing her still dressed as a shepherdess, touched her with her wand, and wished for her the richest dresses that ever were seen. At the word her white cotton frock changed into silver brocade embroidered with carbuncles. From her hair, which was piled high on her head, a long veil of gauze and gold fell down. Her black hair sparkled with diamonds, and her complexion, which had been of dazzling whiteness, became like blooming roses, till the prince could hardly bear to look on its brilliancy. "Ah! Felicity, how beautiful and charming you are!" cried he, with a sigh. "Will you not comfort me in my distress?" "Nay, my son," said the queen, "your cousin will not resist our prayers."

While she was speaking, John passed by on his way to work, and seeing Felicity like a goddess, he thought he must be dreaming. She called him in a kindly voice, and begged the queen to have pity on him. "What! after having ill-treated you so?" she said. "Ah, madam," replied the princess, "I am incapable of revenge." The queen kissed her, praising her generous feeling. "To please you," she added, "I am going to make the ungrateful John rich." Thereupon his hut became a palace, beautifully furnished and full of money. But his stools did not change, neither did his bed, to remind him of his former state. And the Queen of the Woods sharpened his wits, softened his manners, and changed his face. Then John felt capable of gratitude, and poured out his thanks to the queen and the princess.

Afterwards by a touch of her wand, the cabbages became men, and the hen a woman. Only Prince Pink was dissatisfied, and sighed as he stood by his princess, begging her to look more kindly upon him. At last she consented. She had never seen a handsome prince before, and the handsomest was as nothing to this one. The Queen of the Woods, delighted by so happy a marriage, took every pains to make all the arrangements as sumptuous as possible. The merrymaking went on for several years, and the happiness of this loving couple lasted their whole life long.

Babette

THERE was once a queen who had nothing left to wish for but to have children. She could talk of nothing else, and would constantly say that the Fairy Furiosa, who had been present at her birth, and who bore a grudge against the queen, her mother, had flown into a rage, and had wished her nothing but ill-luck.

One day, as she sat alone grieving by the fireside, she saw a little old woman, no bigger than your hand, come down the chimney, riding on three reeds. On her head was a branch of hawthorn; her gown was of flies' wings, and two nutshells served for shoes. She rode through the air, sweeping three times round the room, and then stopped in front of the queen. "For a long time," she said, "you have been grumbling at me, saying I am to blame for your misfortunes, and that I am responsible for all that happens to you. You think, madam, that it is my fault you have no children. I come to announce to you the birth of an infant, but I warn you she will cost you many a tear." "Ah! noble Furiosa," exclaimed the queen, "do not deny me your pity and your aid; I undertake to do everything in my power for you if you will promise that the princess shall be a comfort to me and not a grief." "Fate is stronger than I," replied the fairy. "All that I can do to prove my affection for you is to give you this hawthorn. Fasten it to your daughter's head as soon as she is born; it will protect her from many perils." And, giving her the hawthorn, she vanished like a flash of lightning.

The queen remained sad and pondering. "What!" she said, "do I really desire a daughter who is to cost me many sighs and tears? Should I not be happier without her?" When the king, whom she dearly loved, was with her her troubles seemed more bearable. Her child would soon be born, and in preparation for the event she gave her attendants strict charge to fasten the hawthorn on the princess's head directly she should come into the world. She kept the branch in a golden box covered with diamonds, and valued it above all her possessions.

At length the queen gave birth to the loveliest creature that ever was seen. Without delay the hawthorn was fastened on her head, and at the same instant, wonderful to relate, she turned into a little monkey, and jumped and ran and capered about the room—a perfect monkey and no mistake! At this metamorphosis all the ladies uttered horrible cries, and the queen, more alarmed than any one, thought she should die of despair. She ordered the flowers to be taken off the creature's head. With the greatest difficulty the monkey was caught; but it was in vain that the fatal flowers were removed. She was already a monkey, a confirmed monkey. She could not suck nor do anything else like a child, and cared only about nuts and chestnuts.

"Wicked Furiosa!" exclaimed the queen, sorrowfully, "what have I done that you should treat me so cruelly? What is to become of me? What a disgrace for me, that all my subjects should think I have brought a monster into the world! And how horrified the king will be at seeing such a child!" With tears she entreated her ladies to advise her what to do in this serious case. "Madam," said the oldest, "you must persuade the king that the princess is dead, and we must shut up this monkey in a box and cast it to the bottom of the sea; it would be a terrible thing to keep an animal of this sort any longer."

The queen had some scruple in making up her mind; but when she was told that the king was coming into her room, she became so confused and distressed that without further consideration she bid the lady-in-waiting do what she liked with the monkey.

It was carried into another apartment and shut up in a box. One of the queen's servants was ordered to throw it into the sea;

and he at once set off with it. Now was the princess in the greatest danger; for the man, seeing that the box was beautiful, was very unwilling to throw it away. Sitting down by the sea-shore, he took the monkey out of the box, and, not knowing it was his sovereign, resolved to kill her. But while he held it in his hand a loud noise startled him and made him turn his head. He saw an open chariot drawn by six unicorns, glittering with gold and precious stones, and in front marched several trumpeters. A queen in royal robes and with a crown on her head was seated on cushions of cloth of gold, and held her four-year-old son on her knee.

The servant recognised the queen, for she was his mistress's sister and had come to rejoice with her. But as soon as she learned that the little princess was dead, she set out in great sadness to return to her own kingdom. She was startled from a deep reverie by her son crying out: "I want the monkey! I will have it," and, on looking, the queen saw the prettiest monkey that ever was. The servant looked about for means of escape, but they would not let him go. The queen gave him a large sum of money, and, finding the monkey a gentle little plaything, called her Babette, who thus, in spite of the cruelty of fate, fell into the hands of her aunt.

When she reached her own realms the little prince begged her to give him Babette for a playmate. He wished her to be dressed like a princess; so every day new frocks were made for her. She was taught to walk only on her feet, and a prettier and nicer-looking monkey could nowhere be found. Her face was black as a jay's, and she wore a little white hood with bright red tufts at the ears. Her hands were no bigger than butterflies' wings, and the expression of her bright eyes was so intelligent that no one could be astonished at her accomplishments. When the prince, who was very fond of her, caressed her, as he was always doing, she took great care not to bite him; and when he cried she cried too.

She had been living four years with the queen when, one day, she began to stutter like a child trying to speak. Every one was astonished, and still more so when she began to talk in a sweet and

clear voice, and so distinctly that not a word was lost. Here was a marvel! Babette talking! Babette making herself understood by words! The queen sent for the monkey to amuse her, and, to the great disappointment of the prince, she was taken to the queen's apartment. It cost him some tears, and, to console him, dogs, cats, birds, and squirrels were given him, and even a pony, called Valiant, who knew how to dance but all that did not make up for a word from Babette. As for her, she was less at her ease with the queen than with the prince. She had to reply like a sybil to a hundred witty and learned questions that she did not always understand. Directly an ambassador or a foreigner arrived she had to appear in a gown of velvet or brocade with stiff bodice and ruff. If the court was in mourning she wore a long mantle and crape, a costume that tired her very much. She was no longer permitted to eat what was to her taste: the doctor gave the orders, and these did not at all-please her. She was as self-willed as only a monkey born a princess could be.

The queen gave her masters who cultivated her bright wit. She excelled in playing on the harpsichord; and a wonderful instrument had been made for her out of an oyster-shell. Painters from the four quarters of the globe, and especially from Italy, came to paint her. Her fame flew from one end of the earth to the other, for never before had a talking monkey been heard of.

The prince, as beautiful as Cupid, and as full of grace and wit, was a prodigy no less extraordinary. He came to see Babette, and sometimes played with her; and now and then their talk would turn from merry jests to serious subjects, and to moralising. Babette had a heart; and it had not been metamorphosed like the rest of her little person; and she became so exceedingly fond of the prince that her affection began to be harmful to her. The unhappy Babette did not know what to do. She passed her nights on the top of a window shutter, or in the chimney corner, and would not enter her clean, soft, downy, and padded basket. Her governess (for she had one) heard her often sigh, and sometimes she would utter her laments aloud. Her melancholy grew with her intelligence; and she never saw herself in a mirror without trying in her vexation to break it. For, as it used to be said, once an ape, always an ape, so Babette could not get rid of the evil disposition natural to her race.

The prince had grown up. He liked hunting, dancing, the drama, feats of arms, and books, and rarely now gave the monkey a thought. With her it was quite otherwise. She loved him better at twelve than she had at six; but when she reproached him for his neglect he thought he made the amplest amends that could to be expected of him when he gave her a rosy apple or some candied chestnuts.

At last the fame of Babette began to make a great sensation in Monkeyland, and Magot, the king of the monkeys, was greatly desirous of marrying her. For that purpose he sent a magnificent embassy to ask her hand from the queen. It was not difficult to explain his intentions to his chief ministers, but it would have been infinitely hard to express them to others without the aid of parrots and the birds commonly called magpies. They chattered a great deal; and the jays, who accompanied the procession, felt in honour bound to make as much noise as their companions.

A big ape, called Gregory, was chief of the embassy. He had a coach made of pasteboard, on which were painted the loves of the King Magot with Monette, a monkey renowned throughout Monkeyland, who had died a cruel death by the claws of a wild cat that had taken her playfulness seriously. The delights that Magot and Monette had enjoyed during their married life, and the profound sorrow with which the king had wept for her after her death, were there depicted. Six white rabbits, of first-rate breed, drew the coach, called by distinction the state carriage. Behind came a chariot, in which were the monkeys destined to wait on Babette. You should have seen how they were dressed! It really seemed as if they were going to a wedding. The rest of the procession was composed of little spaniels, young greyhounds,

Spanish cats, Muscovy rats, a few hedgehogs, sly weasels, and greedy foxes. Some drove the chariots, others carried the baggage. Gregory, graver than a Roman dictator, rode a young hare, that ambled better than an English gelding.

The queen knew nothing of this magnificent embassy until it arrived at her palace. Hearing shouts of laughter from the people and the guards she put her head out of the window, and beheld the most extraordinary cavalcade she had ever seen in her life. Immediately Gregory, followed by a considerable number of monkeys, approached the chariot of the ladies of his troop, and, giving his paw to the big one, called Gigona, he helped her to get down. Then letting loose the little parrot, who was to act as his interpreter, he waited while the beautiful bird was presented to the queen and begged an audience.

The parrot, mounting gently in the air, went to the window from which the queen was looking out, and said in the prettiest tone of voice imaginable: "Madam, his grace Count Gregory, ambassador of the celebrated Magot, king of Monkeyland, begs an audience of your majesty, to discuss a very important question." "Pretty parrot," said the queen, caressing him, "first you must eat some roast meat and have something to drink. After that, you may go and tell Count Gregory that he is heartily welcome to my realm, and so are all who accompany him. If he is not too much fatigued by his journey, he can presently enter the audience chamber, where I, on my throne, will await him with the whole court."

At these words the parrot kissed his claw twice, saluted the guard, sang a little tune to give vent to his joy, and taking to his wings again and perching on Gregory's shoulder, whispered in his ear the favourable answer he had just received. Gretory was fully sensible of the honour, and told the magpie Mary, who had been appointed as sub-interpreter, to ask one of the queen's officers to be good enough to give him a room in which to rest for a few moments. Accordingly, a saloon paved with coloured and gilded marble, one of the handsomest in the palace, was opened, and he entered with a part of his suite. But since monkeys are naturally very inquisitive, they smelt out a certain corner in which many pots of preserves had been stored. Immediately the gluttons set on it. One seized a crystal cup full of apricots, another a bottle of syrup; some took patties, others marzipan. The winged creatures who accompanied them were vexed at the sight of a repast where there was neither hemp nor millet seed; and a jay, by profession a great talker, flew into the audience chamber and, respectfully approaching the queen, said: "Madam, I am too much your majesty's obedient servant to be a willing party to the havoc that is being made in your delicious preserves. Count Gregory has already eaten three pots himself; he was gobbling up the fourth without the slightest respect for your royal majesty when, deeply grieved, I came to warn you." "Many thanks, little jay, for your friendly thought," said the queen, smiling, "but you need not be so zealous for my pots of preserves; I relinquish them for the sake of Babette, whom I love with all my heart." The jay, somewhat ashamed of the attack he had just made, withdrew without a word.

A few moments later the ambassador entered, accompanied by his suite. He was not dressed quite in the fashion, for since the famous Francis, who made such a brilliant figure in the world, had returned home, a good model had been lacking. He wore a sugar-loaf hat with a bunch of green feathers, a shoulder-belt of blue paper covered with gold spangles, deep frills to his breeches, and carried a cane. The parrot, who passed for something of a poet, having composed a very solemn harangue, advanced to the foot of the throne on which the queen was seated. Addressing Babette, he spoke thus:

"Learn the power of your eyes' bright fire
By the love that they in King Magot inspire!
These monkeys, birds, cats—all this splendid array
Are here, at his word, and his passion display.
Monette, the queen, beloved of her race—
Except you, none had ever so comely a face—
By a wild cat's claws she was mangled and torn,
And Magot, the king, was left all forlorn.
The king to her memory faithfulness swore,
And to love her for ever and evermore;
But you, from his heart, by your sweet perfection,
Have chased of his first love all recollection.
In you now, madam, he finds all his delight;
And, could you but measure his passion's height,
No doubt but your heart, framed in pity's fashion
To cure his love, would share his passion.
For once on a time he was hearty and gay,
But now he is weak and thin alway

As if pain bore him company every hour—
Ah! madam, indeed he feels love's power!
The olives and nuts that he found so good
Are now to his palate but tasteless food;
He dies!—'tis you alone that can save—
You alone can keep him on this side the grave.
On all the delights that your coming await
In our happy land, can I not dilate.
There figs and grapes will fail you never,
And the finest fruits are in season ever."

The parrot had no sooner finished his speech than the queen looked at Babette, who was covered with confusion. Before replying, the queen, wishing to find out her feelings, asked the parrot to explain to the ambassador that, as far as she was concerned, she favoured his master's suit. The audience finished, she withdrew, and Babette followed her into her closet. "My little one," she said, "I shall be very sorry to part with you, but it is not possible to refuse Magot, who asks your hand in marriage, for I have not yet forgotten that his father sent two hundred thousand monkeys into the field to carry on a great war against mine. They ate so many of our subjects that we were obliged to make an ignominious peace." "You mean, madam," answered Babette, impatiently, "that, to avoid his wrath, you are resolved to sacrifice me to this wretched monster, but I at least implore your majesty to grant me a few days in which to make up my mind." "That is but fair," said the queen. "Nevertheless, if you will take my advice, decide quickly. Consider the honours in store for you, the magnificence of the embassy, and the number of ladies-in-waiting sent to you. I am sure that Magot never did for Monette what he has done for you." "I do not know what he did for Monette," replied little Babette, disdainfully, "but I do know that I care very little for these marks of affection for me." Then she rose, and, gracefully curtseying, sought the prince to tell him her troubles. As soon as he saw her, he cried out: "Well, my Babette, when are we to dance at your wedding?" "I do not know, sir," she said sadly, "but I am so wretched that I have no longer the strength to keep my secret from you; and, although it ill becomes my modesty, I must confess to you that you are the only one I wish for a husband." "Husband!" said the prince, bursting out laughing, "husband, little one! Well, that is delightful! But all the same, I trust you will excuse me if I do not accept your proposal, for, to tell the truth, in our persons, our appearance, and our manners, we are not exactly a match." "I agree with you," she said, "especially since our hearts are not alike. For a long while I have seen that you are ungrateful, and I am extremely foolish to love a prince who so little deserves it." "But, Babette," said he, "think of the trouble I should be in to see you perched on the top of a sycamore, holding on to a branch by the end of your tail. Come now, let this be a joke, and for your honour and mine marry the monkey king and, in token of our firm friendship, send me your first little baby." "It is fortunate for you, sir, that my nature is not entirely that of a monkey. Any other than myself would have already torn out your eyes, bitten off your nose, and wrenched off your ears; but I leave you to the reflections your unworthy conduct will one day cause you." She could say no more. Her governess came to fetch her, the ambassador Gregory having entered her apartment with magnificent presents.

There was a costume made of a spider's web, embroidered with glowworms, and an egg-shell case for combs. A white-heart cherry served for a pincushion, and all the linen was trimmed with paper lace. In a basket there were several carefully-chosen shells, some to serve for ear-rings, others for bodkins, all of them shining like diamonds; and, what was even better, a dozen boxes full of sweetmeats, and a little glass chest with a hazel-nut and an olive inside. But the key of this was lost, and Babette troubled little about it.

The ambassador gave her to understand, in the chattering

language of Monkeyland, that his sovereign was more touched by her charms than he had ever been by those of any other monkey; that he intended to build her a palace at the top of a fir tree; that he sent these gifts and the fine preserves as a mark of his attachment; and that indeed the king, his master, could prove his affection in no better way. "But," he added, "the strongest testimony to his love, and that which you ought to feel most deeply, is, madam, the trouble he has been to have his picture painted, so that you may anticipate the pleasure of seeing him." He then displayed the portrait of the King of the Monkeys, seated on a huge log, eating an apple.

Babette turned away her head that she might not look longer on so ugly a face, and after some little display of temper gave Gregory to understand that she thanked his master for his esteem, but that, as yet, she had not made up her mind whether she intended to marry at all.

Meanwhile, the queen determined not to draw down on herself the anger of the monkeys, and, believing there would be little difficulty in sending Babette wherever she wished her to go, had everything prepared for her departure. At this news, despair took possession of Babette. The prince's disdain on one hand, the queen's indifference on the other, and more than all that, the prospect of such a husband, made her resolve to run away. It was not a very difficult matter for, since she could speak, she was no longer tied up, and came and went as she liked, and would enter her room as often by the window as by the door.

She set out as quickly as possible, jumping from tree to tree, from branch to branch, until she came to the bank of a river. The violence of her despair blinded her to the danger she was running into in attempting to cross by swimming. Without the least consideration she threw herself in, and immediately went to the bottom. But there she did not lose consciousness; she saw a magnificent grotto, adorned with shells. She hastened in, and was received by a venerable old man, whose white beard reached to his waist. He was lying on a bed of reeds and irises, with a crown of poppies and wild lilies on his head, and propped up against a rock, from whence flowed several springs that fed the river.

"Well! what brings you here, my little Babette?" said he, reaching her his hand. "Sir," she replied, "I am an unfortunate monkey; I am running away from a hideous ape, to whom they wish to marry me." "I know more about you than you think," said the wise old man. "It is true you detest Magot, but it is equally true that you love a young prince who cares nothing for you." "Ah! sir," cried Babette, sighing, "do not let us speak of him. The recollection of him only makes my sorrows harder to bear." "He

will not be always insensible to love," continued the King of the Fish. "I know he is reserved for the most beautiful princess in the world." "Unhappy wretch that I am!" continued Babette. "Then he will never be mine!" The old man smiled, and said: "Do not grieve, my good Babette. Time is a wonderful master. Only take care not to lose the little glass chest Magot sent you, and that you have, perchance, now in your pocket. I can tell you no more. Here is a tortoise that travels at a good rate. Seat yourself on her; she will take you where you have to go." "After what I owe you," said Babette, "I cannot help wishing to know your name." "I am called," he said, "Biroquoi, father of Biroquie, a river, as you see, of considerable size and fame."

Babette mounted her tortoise with the greatest confidence. For a long time they floated over the water, and at length, by what seemed a very roundabout way, the tortoise gained the bank. It would be difficult to imagine anything prettier than her side saddle and the rest of the trappings. There were even little horse-pistols, for which two crab-shells served as cases.

Babette was journeying on with the utmost confidence in wise Biroquoi's promises when she suddenly heard a great noise. Alas! alas! It was the ambassador Gregory, with all his attendants, returning to Monkeyland, sad and sorrowful at Babette's flight. A monkey belonging to the troop had, during the halt for dinner, climbed a nut tree, in order to throw down nuts to feed the little ones. No sooner had he reached the top of the tree than, looking round on every side, he saw Babette on the poor tortoise, who was slowly making her way across the open country. At sight of her he began to shout so loudly that the assembled monkeys asked him, in their language, what was the matter. He told them, and immediately the magpies and jays were let loose, and they flew to where she was. On their report, the ambassador, the monkeys, and the rest of the company ran and stopped her.

Here was a misfortune for Babette! Nothing more unlucky or disagreeable could possibly have happened. She was forced to get

into the state carriage, which was immediately surrounded by the most vigilant monkeys, by a few foxes, and a cock who, perched on the top, kept guard day and night. A monkey led the tortoise along as a rare animal, and so the cavalcade continued its journey, to the great sorrow of Babette, whose sole companion was Madam Gigona, a cross-grained and disagreeable monkey.

At the end of three days, which passed without adventure, the guides having lost their way, they reached a large and magnificent city, whose name they did not know. Seeing a beautiful garden with the gate standing open, they stopped there, and plundered it, as if it had been a conquered country. One crunched nuts, another gobbled cherries, a third despoiled a plum tree. Indeed, there was not the smallest monkey but joined in the pillage, and laid in a store.

You must know that this city was the capital of the kingdom where Babette was born. Her mother lived there and, since she had had the misfortune to see her daughter changed into a monkey by means of a hawthorn branch, had never allowed a monkey, a baboon, or an ape to remain in the kingdom, nor, indeed, anything that could recall to her mind the deplorable and fatal circumstance. A monkey was looked upon as a disturber of the public peace. Think, then, what was the astonishment of the people to see a pasteboard coach, a chariot of painted straw, and all the rest of the most extraordinary cavalcade that was ever seen since tales were tales, and fairies fairies!

The news spread quickly to the palace. The queen was paralysed; she thought the whole race of monkeys meant to make an attack on her government. She immediately summoned her council, who, by her orders, found the whole troop guilty of high treason, and, not wishing to lose the opportunity of making such an example of them as should be remembered in the future, she sent her officers into the garden with orders to seize them all. Big nets were cast over the trees, and the capture was soon effected.

In spite of the respect due to the rank of an ambassador, this high office was most contemptuously treated in the person of Gregory. He was pitilessly cast into the depths of a cellar under a big empty cask, where he and his companions were imprisoned, with the lady monkeys, both matrons and damsels, who accompanied Babette.

As for Babette, she felt a secret joy at this fresh disturbance. When misfortunes reach a certain point nothing further is dreaded, and death itself seems desirable. Such was her condition, for her heart was full of the prince who disdained her, and her mind occupied with the horrible thought of King Magot, whose wife she was on the point of becoming.

Besides, we must not forget to mention that she was so prettily dressed, and her manners were so distinguished, that those who had seized her, stopped to look at her as something quite marvellous, and when she spoke to them they were still more surprised, for they had already heard of the wonderful Babette. The queen who had found her, and who did not know of her niece's metamorphosis, had often written to her sister that she possessed an extraordinary monkey, and begged her to come and see it, but the unhappy queen would pass over that sentence without reading it.

At length the warders, carried away by admiration, brought Babette into a big gallery and made her a little throne. She sat on it more like a sovereign than a captive monkey, and the queen, happening to pass by, was so vastly taken with her pretty face and the charming compliments she paid her, that, in spite of herself, the nature within her made appeal for the infant. She took her in her arms; and, as for the little creature, feelings she had never known before stirred within her. She threw herself on the queen's neck and spoke such loving and engaging words that all who heard her were delighted. "No, madam," she exclaimed, "it is not the fear of approaching death, with which I am told you threaten the unfortunate race of monkeys, that terrifies me and makes me try to please you and soften your heart. The cutting short of my life is by no means the greatest misfortune that can happen to me, and I have in me feelings so far above my condition that I should regret any step whatsoever that might be taken to preserve my life. It is you yourself I love. Your crown is of far less consequence to me than your goodness."

I ask you, what reply could be made when Babette spoke such winning words? The queen said not a word, but opened her two eyes wide, seemed to consider, and felt her heart strangely stirred.

She carried the monkey into her room, and when they were alone she said to her: "Tell me your adventures without a moment's delay, for I feel that of all the animals who inhabit the menageries, and whom I keep in my palace, you will be the one I shall love most. I assure you that for your sake I will pardon the monkeys who accompany you." "Ah! madam," she exclaimed, "I ask nothing for them. By ill-luck I was born a monkey, and that same ill-luck gave me intelligence that will cause me suffering till I die. For what must I feel when I see myself in my mirror: little, ugly, and sooty, my hands covered with hair, with a tail, and with teeth ever ready to bite; while, at the same time, I do not lack intelligence, and have taste, refinement, and quick feelings?" "Do you know what it is to love?" said the queen. Babette sighed, but did not answer. "Oh!" continued the queen, "you must tell me if you love a monkey, a rabbit, or a squirrel; for, if you are not already too deeply pledged, I have a dwarf who will just suit you." At that proposal Babette looked so disdainful that the queen burst out laughing. "Don't be angry," she said, "and tell me how it is that you can speak."

"All that I know of my adventures," replied Babette, "is that your sister had scarcely left you after the birth and death of your daughter, when going along the sea-shore she saw one of your servants on the point of drowning me. At her command I was taken from him. By a miracle, that equally astonished everybody, speech and reason were given to me. Masters, who taught me several languages and to play musical instruments, were provided for me. At length, madam, I became aware of my misfortune, and – but," she exclaimed, seeing the queen's face pale and covered with a cold perspiration, "what is the matter, madam? I observe an extraordinary change in your appearance." "I am dying!" said the queen, in a weak, almost inaudible voice, "I am dying; my beloved and only too unhappy daughter! I have at last found you again!" At these words she swooned. Babette, terrified, ran and called for aid. The queen's ladies hurried to give her water, to unlace her and put her to bed. Babette crept in with her, and she was so small that no one noticed her.

When the queen had recovered from the long swoon into which the princess's words had thrown her, she desired to be left alone with the ladies who knew the fatal secret of her daughter's birth. She told them what had happened, and they were so dismayed that they did not know what advice to give.

But the queen commanded them to tell her what they considered it expedient to do in this lamentable case. Some said the monkey must be strangled, others that she should be shut up in a den; others, even that she should be again thrown into the sea. The queen wept and sobbed. "She has so much intelligence," said she, "what a pity to see her reduced to this miserable condition by an enchanted bouquet! But, after all," continued she, "she is my daughter; it is I who brought on her the wicked Furiosa's anger. Is it right that she should suffer on account of that fairy's hatred for me?" "Yes, madam," exclaimed her old lady-in-waiting, "your reputation must be saved. What would the world think if you declared that a little monkey was your daughter? It's not in nature to have such children when one is as beautiful as you." The queen lost patience at hearing her talk thus. But the old lady and the others were equally persistent that the little monster must be got rid of; and, finally, she determined to shut Babette up in a castle, where she would be well fed and kindly treated for the rest of her life.

When Babette heard that the queen intended to put her in

prison, she slipped quietly out by the side of the bed, and, throwing herself from the window on to a tree in the garden, escaped to the big forest, and left everybody in confusion at her loss.

She spent the night in the hollow of an oak, where she had leisure to reflect on the cruelty of her fate. What caused her most distress was to be forced to leave the queen; but she preferred voluntary exile and the preservation of her liberty to the loss of it for ever.

As soon as it was light she continued her journey, without knowing where she wished to go, thinking and thinking a thousand times over of the strangeness of this most extraordinary adventure. "What a difference," she exclaimed, "between what I am and what I was meant to be!" Tears flowed freely from poor Babette's little eyes.

Directly day appeared she set out, fearing the queen would send after her, or that one of the monkeys escaped from the cellar would take her, against her will, to King Magot. She went on by slow degrees without following road or path until she reached a great desert, where there was neither house, nor tree, nor fruit, nor grass, nor spring. She entered it without thinking and, only when she began to feel hungry, recognised too late that travelling in such a country was exceedingly imprudent.

Two days and two nights went by without her being able to catch even a grub or a fly. The fear of death seized on her, and she was so weak that she was on the point of swooning. She sank down on the ground and, remembering the olive and the hazel nut in the little glass box, she thought they might make her a slight repast. Delighted at this ray of hope, she took a stone, broke the box to pieces, and crunched the olive.

But she had scarcely put her teeth in it when a great quantity of scented oil came pouring out upon her paws, which turned into the most beautiful hands in the world. Her surprise was extreme: she took the oil and rubbed herself all over. Oh, wondrous. She immediately became so beautiful that there was nothing in the world like her. She felt that she had big eyes, a small mouth and a well-shaped nose. She was dying for a mirror, and at length managed to improvise one out of the biggest piece of the glass box. And when she saw herself, what joy! What a delightful surprise! Her clothes grew in size like herself; her head was well dressed; her hair fell in thousands of curls; her complexion was fresh as the flowers in spring. The first moments of surprise over, hunger made itself more acutely felt, and her distress vastly

increased. "What!" she said, "so young and so beautiful, a born princess, and I must perish in this barren place! Oh! wretched fate that led me here! How strangely is my destiny shaped! Have you made so delightful and unexpected a change in me only to make my troubles greater? And you, venerable River Biroquie, who so generously saved my life, will you leave me to perish in this frightful solitude?"

In vain did the princess implore help – the whole world was deaf to her voice. Hunger tormented her to such a degree that she took the hazel nut and cracked it. In throwing away the shell, she was greatly surprised to see come out of it architects, painters, masons, upholsterers, sculptors, and ever so many other sorts of workmen. Some made designs for a palace, others built it; others, again, furnished it. Some decorated the rooms, and some cultivated the gardens; everything shone with gold and azure. A magnificent banquet was served. Sixty princesses, more beautifully dressed than queens, accompanied by squires and followed by pages, came to her with charming compliments, and invited her to the feast that awaited her. Babette at once, without waiting to be entreated, advanced quickly, with the air of a queen, into the hall, where she ate ravenously of the food.

Scarcely had she left the table when her treasurers brought her fifteen thousand chests, big as hogsheads, filled with gold and diamonds. They asked her if she was agreeable that they should pay the workmen who had built her palace. She replied that was only right, on condition that they would also build a city, marry, and remain with her. They all consented and, although the city was five times bigger than Rome, it was finished in three quarters of an hour. Surely these were wonders enough to come out of a little hazel nut!

The princess was considering in her mind whether she should send an imposing embassy to her mother, and some reproachful messages to her cousin, the young prince. While the necessary measures were being taken she amused herself with looking on at the tilting, where she always awarded the prize, with cards, the play, hunting and fishing, for a river had been brought into her domain. The fame of her beauty spread over the whole world: kings from the four corners of the earth came to her court with giants taller than mountains, and pigmies smaller than rats.

It happened that on a certain day a great tournament was being held. Several knights entered the lists. They got angry with each other, came to blows, and were wounded. The princess, in great wrath, came down from the balcony to see who were the guilty men: but when they were disarmed, what was her distress to see the prince, her cousin! If he was not dead, he was very nearly so, and she thought she must herself die of surprise and grief. She had him carried into the finest apartment of the palace, where nothing necessary for his cure was wanting—physicians from Chodrai, surgeons, salves, broths, and syrups. Babette herself made the bandages and prepared the lint. Her eyes moistened them with tears, and such tears must have been balm to the sick man. For, indeed, he was ill in more ways than one; not to reckon a half-dozen sword thrusts, and as many cuts from a lance which pierced him right through, he had been for some time at the court *incognito,* and had fallen a victim to the power of Babette's charms to an extent past recovery. It is then easy to imagine something of what he now felt, when he could read in the kindly princess's face that she was in the utmost trouble because of the condition to which he was reduced.

I shall not stop to record all the things his heart prompted him to say in thanking her for the kindness she showed him. Those who heard him were surprised that a man so ill could show so much affection and gratitude. Babette, who blushed more than once, begged him to be silent; but the emotion and the ardour of his words excited him to such an extent that she saw him suddenly seized by a frightful agony. Until then she had remained perfectly calm, but now she entirely lost her self-control, tore her hair, uttered loud cries, and made everybody think that her heart was

easily given away, since, in this short time, she had become so fond of a stranger. For in Babette (as she had called her kingdom) it was not known that the prince was her cousin, and that she had loved him since her childhood.

It was while travelling that he had stopped at her court, and, as he knew no one to present him to the princess, he thought nothing would serve him better than to perform before her five or six heroic feats: for instance, to cut off the legs and arms of the knights of the tournament. But he did not find them amiable enough to permit this. There was only in consequence a wild confusion; the strongest overcame the weakest, and, as I have already said, the weakest was the prince.

Babette, in despair, ran along the high road without carriage or guards. Entering a wood, she fell swooning at the foot of a tree, where the Fairy Furiosa, who never slept, and only sought opportunities of doing evil, came and carried her off in a cloud which was blacker than ink, and travelled faster than the wind. For some time the princess remained unconscious, but at length she came to herself. Never did surprise equal hers at finding herself so far from the earth, and so near the heavens. The floor of the cloud was not solid, so that in running here and there she seemed to be walking on feathers, and when it partly opened she had much ado to keep from falling off. There was no one to whom she could complain, for the wicked Furiosa had made herself invisible. She had time to think of her beloved prince, and of the condition in which she had left him, and her soul was filled with the saddest thoughts. "How!" she exclaimed, "can I survive him whom I love, or how can dread of a speedy death find a place in my heart! Ah! If the sun would scorch me it would be doing me a good turn, or if I could drown myself in the rainbow, how happy I should be! But, alas, the whole zodiac is deaf to my cries: the archer has no arrows, the bull no horns, the lion no teeth. Perhaps the earth will be kinder, and on the sharp point of a rock I may meet my death. Oh, prince, my beloved cousin, if you were only here to see me take the most tragic leap a despairing lover can imagine." With these words she ran to the edge of the cloud, and threw herself off like an arrow shot from a tight-strung bow.

All who saw her thought the moon was falling; and as the moon was then on the wane, many of its worshippers, who were to be some time without seeing it again, went into deep mourning, and persuaded themselves that the sun had played it this wicked trick out of jealousy.

However desirous the princess might be of dying, she did not succeed. She fell into the glass bottle in which the fairies generally exposed their wine to the sun. But what a bottle! No tower in the universe was so big! Fortunately it was empty, or she would have been drowned like a fly.

The six giants who guarded it immediately recognised her. They were the same who dwelt in her court, and they loved her. The malicious Furiosa, who did nothing by chance, had transported them there each on his winged dragon, and when the giants slept the dragons guarded the bottle. While Babette was there, there were many days when she regretted the loss of her monkey's skin. She lived like the chameleons on air and dew.

The princess's prison was known to none. The prince was ignorant of its existence. He was not dead, and continually asked for Babette. He saw by the melancholy of all those who attended him that there was some cause of general grief at the court. His native good-breeding prevented him from seeking to discover it. But when he was convalescent he begged so hard for news of the princess that they had not the courage to conceal her loss from him. Those who had seen her enter the wood declared she had been devoured by lions, and others believed she had killed herself out of despair; others again maintained that she had gone out of her mind, and was wandering over the world.

Since the last suggestion was the least terrible, and somewhat revived the prince's hopes, he decided it was so, and set out on Valiant, whom I mentioned before—although I did not remark

that he was the eldest son of Bucephalus, and one of the best horses of that age. Riding with a loose rein, letting his horse go at hazard, he called Babette's name aloud, but the echoes alone replied.

At length he reached the bank of a broad river. Valiant was thirsty, and went into the water to drink; and the prince, according to his custom, began to shout with all his might: "Babette, beautiful Babette, where are you?"

He heard a voice whose sweetness seemed to delight the wave; it said to him: "Approach, and you shall know where she is." At those words the prince, as brave as he was loving, gave two pricks of the spur to Valiant, swam out and found a gulf where the water rushed down more rapidly. He sank to the bottom, fully persuaded that he was going to be drowned.

He arrived safely at the abode of the good Biroquoi, who was celebrating his daughter's marriage with one of the richest and most important rivers of the land. All the fishy deities were in the grotto; tritons and mermaids made pleasant music, and the River Biroquie, lightly clad, danced with the Seine, the Thames, the Euphrates, and the Ganges, who had certainly come a long way to enjoy each other's society. Valiant, who was a well-bred horse, stopped respectfully at the entrance of the grotto, and the prince, whose manners were even better than those of his horse, making a low bow, asked if a mortal like himself was permitted to appear among so fine a company.

Biroquoi took up the word, and replied in an affable manner that they would be honoured and pleased were he to do so. "I have been expecting you, sir, for some days," he continued. "I am devoted to your interests, and those of Babette are dear to me. You must rescue her from the fatal place where the vindictive Furiosa has imprisoned her. She is shut up in a bottle." "What do you tell me!" exclaimed the prince, "the princess in a bottle?" "Yes," said the wise old man, "she suffers greatly; but I warn you, sir, that unless you follow my advice it is not easy to overcome the giants and dragons who guard her. You must leave your good horse here, and mount a winged dolphin I have been training for you for a long time past." He ordered the dolphin, saddled and bridled, to be brought, and it pranced and danced so finely that Valiant was jealous.

Biroquoi and his companions made haste to arm the prince. They put on him shining armour made of the scales of golden carps; his helmet was a big snail-shell, shaded by a large cod's tail, raised up to form an aigrette; a mermaid girded him with an eel belt, from which hung a formidable sword made of a long fish bone. Afterwards he was given a great tortoise-shell for a shield; and so equipped there was never a little gudgeon that would not have taken him for the god of the soles, for, to speak the truth, this young prince had a certain air seldom found among mortals.

The hope of soon finding the charming princess he loved inspired him with a gladness he had been unable to feel since her disappearance, and the faithful chronicler of this tale remarks that he ate with a good appetite at Biroquoi's board, and thanked the company in no common words. He bade his Valiant farewell, and mounted the flying fish, which immediately set out.

At the end of the day the prince found himself so high up that, in order to rest a little, he entered the kingdom of the moon. The strange and rare things he discovered there would have delighted him had he been less anxious to get his Babette out of the bottle in which she had been living for several months.

Day had scarcely dawned when he saw her surrounded by the giants and dragons that the fairy, by the power of her wand, had set over her. So little did the fairy dream that any one could be strong enough to deliver her, that she relied on the vigilance of her terrible guards to keep her in suffering.

The beautiful princess was pitifully looking at the heavens, and addressing her sad laments to them, when she saw the flying dolphin and knight who came to rescue her. She would not have believed the adventure possible had she not known, from her own experience, that to certain people the most extraordinary things are always happening. "Is this knight," she said, "transported into the air by the malice of the fairies? Alas! How I pity him if a bottle or a decanter is to serve him for a prison, like me!"

While she was reflecting thus, the giants, who saw the prince above their heads, thought it was a kite, and cried one to the other: "Catch it; catch the cord, it will amuse us." But when they stooped to pick it up, he cut and thrust at them, and hacked them to pieces like a pack of cards you cut in half and scatter to the winds. At the noise of this great combat the princess turned her head and recognised her young prince. What joy to be certain he still lived, but what terror to see him in so evident danger in the midst of those terrible giants and dragons who were throwing themselves on him! She cried aloud in terror, and the thought of the danger he was in nearly killed her.

However, the magic fish bone with which Biroquoi had armed the prince's hand did not strike in vain, and the nimble dolphin, who raised himself, and came down just at the right moment, was also a wonderful help; so that in a very short time the ground was covered with the monsters.

The impatient prince, seeing his Babette through the glass, would have dashed it in pieces had he not feared wounding her. So he descended instead by the neck of the bottle. When he was at the bottom he threw himself at Babette's feet and respectfully kissed her hand. "Sir," said she, "it is right, if I am to deserve your esteem, that I should tell you the reasons that induced me to take so tender an interest in your preservation. You must know that we are near relations, that I am the daughter of the queen, your aunt, and the very same Babette you found in the shape of a monkey by the sea-shore, and who afterwards was weak enough to show towards you an affection you disdained." "Ah, madam!" exclaimed the prince. "Can I believe so extraordinary a tale? You were a monkey! You loved me! I knew it; and my heart was capable of refusing the greatest happiness in the world!" "I should now," replied the princess, smiling, "have a very poor opinion of your

taste if you could then have felt any affection for me. But, sir, let us depart; I am tired of being a prisoner, and I fear my enemy. Let us go to the queen, my mother, and tell her these extraordinary things, that must surely be of great interest to her." "Come, let us go, madam," said the anxious prince, mounting his winged dolphin, and taking her in his arms. "Let us restore to her, in your person, the most charming princess in the world."

The dolphin rose up gently, and shaped his course towards the capital, where the queen was passing her sad life. Babette's flight had left her not a moment of peace. She could not help thinking of her and recalling the pretty things she had said to her; and, monkey as she was, the queen would have given half her kingdom to see Babette again.

When the prince arrived he disguised himself as an old man and asked for a private audience. "Madam," he said, "since my earliest youth I have studied the art of necromancy. You must know, therefore, that I am not ignorant of the hatred Furiosa has for you, and the terrible results it has caused. But dry your tears, madam; Babette, whom you remember so ugly, is now the most beautiful princess in the world. You will soon have her with you if you will forgive the queen, your sister, for the cruel war she has waged against you, and conclude the peace by the marriage of your daughter with your nephew, the prince." "I cannot delude myself that what you tell me is true," replied the queen, weeping. "Good old man, you wish to alleviate my distress; I have lost my daughter, I have no longer a husband; my sister claims my kingdom, her son is as unjust as she is, they persecute me; I will never make an alliance with them." "Fate decrees otherwise," he continued; "I am chosen to inform you of it." "Well, and where would be the good, if I did consent to this marriage? The wicked Furiosa has too much power and malice; she would never be reconciled to it." "Do not disturb yourself about that, madam," replied the old man; "only promise me that you will offer no opposition to the desired marriage." "I promise everything," exclaimed the queen, "if only I may see my beloved daughter once more."

The prince left her, and ran to the spot where Babette was waiting for him. She was surprised at his disguise, and he was obliged to tell her that for some time the interests of the two queens had been greatly opposed, and that there had been much ill-feeling between them, but that he had just gained his aunt's consent to what he wished. The princess was enchanted. She repaired to the palace, and all who looked on her saw in her so perfect a likeness to her mother that they eagerly followed to find out who she was.

As soon as the queen saw her, her heart was so mightily stirred that no other testimony was needed to the truth of the story. The princess threw herself at the feet of the queen, who clasped her in her arms. At first they were silent, wiping away each other's tears with a thousand tender kisses; and then they said everything that such an occasion could suggest. Then the queen, casting her eyes on her nephew, welcomed him very kindly, and repeated to him what she had promised the magician. She would have gone on speaking, but, hearing a noise in the courtyard of the palace, she put her head out of the window, and had the pleasant surprise of seeing that the queen, her sister, had arrived. The prince and the princess, who were looking out, recognised in her suite the venerable Biroquoi; and even the good Valiant was there too. Each party shouted for joy at the sight of the other; and they hastened to meet once again with a delight that cannot be described. The far-famed marriage of the prince and the princess was immediately concluded in defiance of the Fairy Furiosa, whose cunning and malice were thus equally confounded.